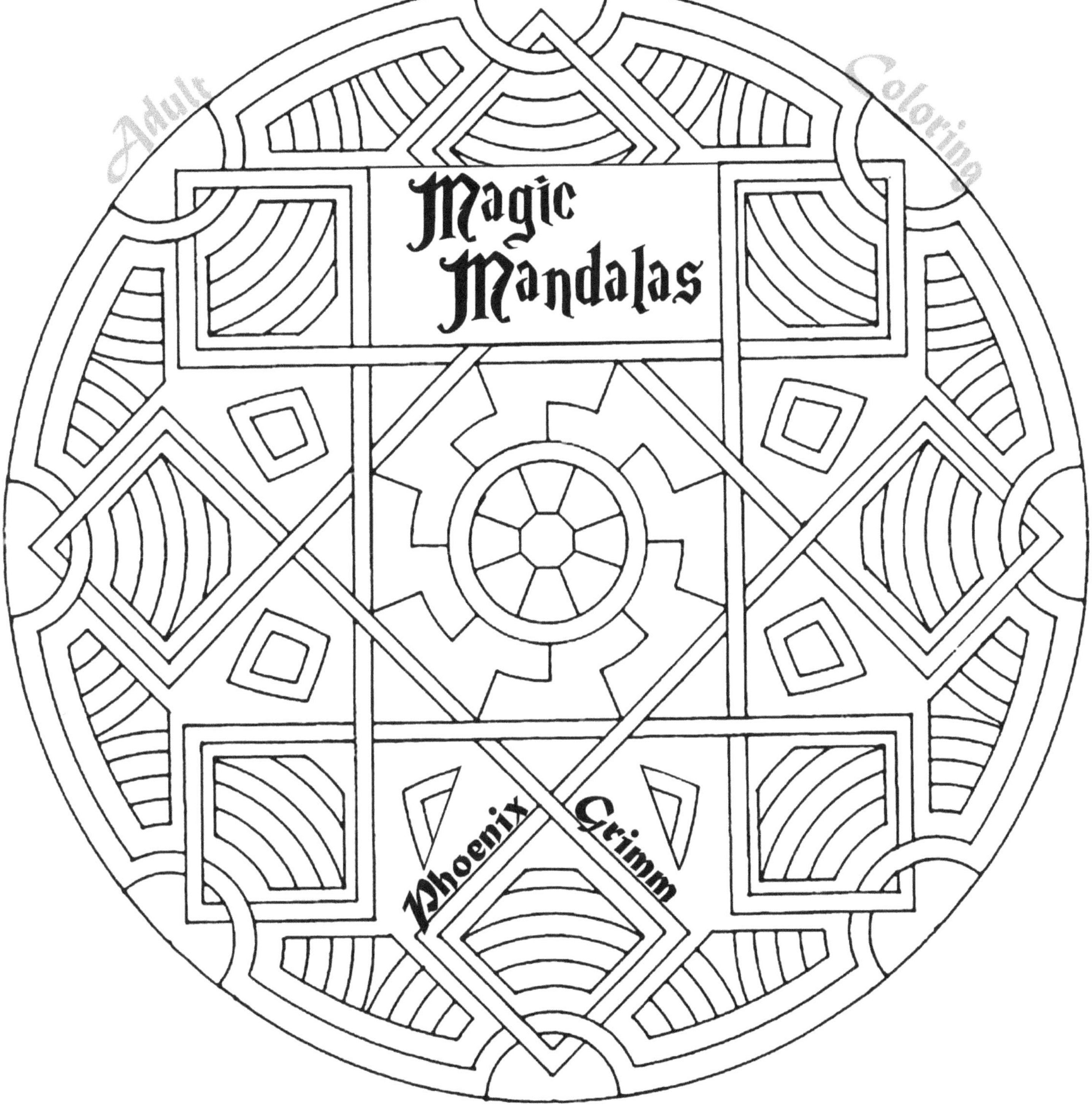
Adult
Coloring
Magic
Mandalas
Phoenix
Grimm

ISBN: 1523999780

ISBN-13: 978-1523999781

See more from the author and print free pages at

www.facebook.com/phoenix.ink.coloring/

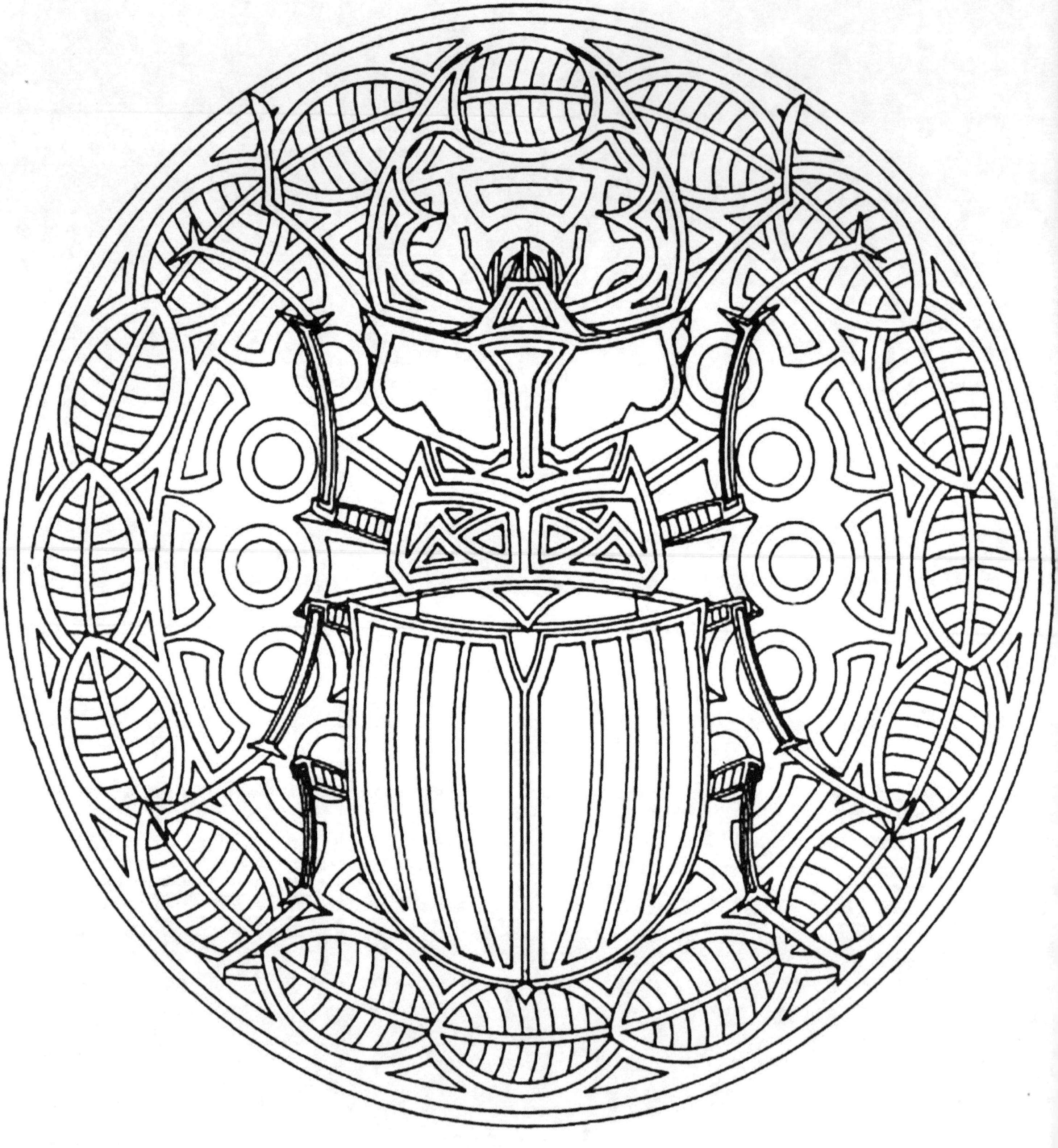

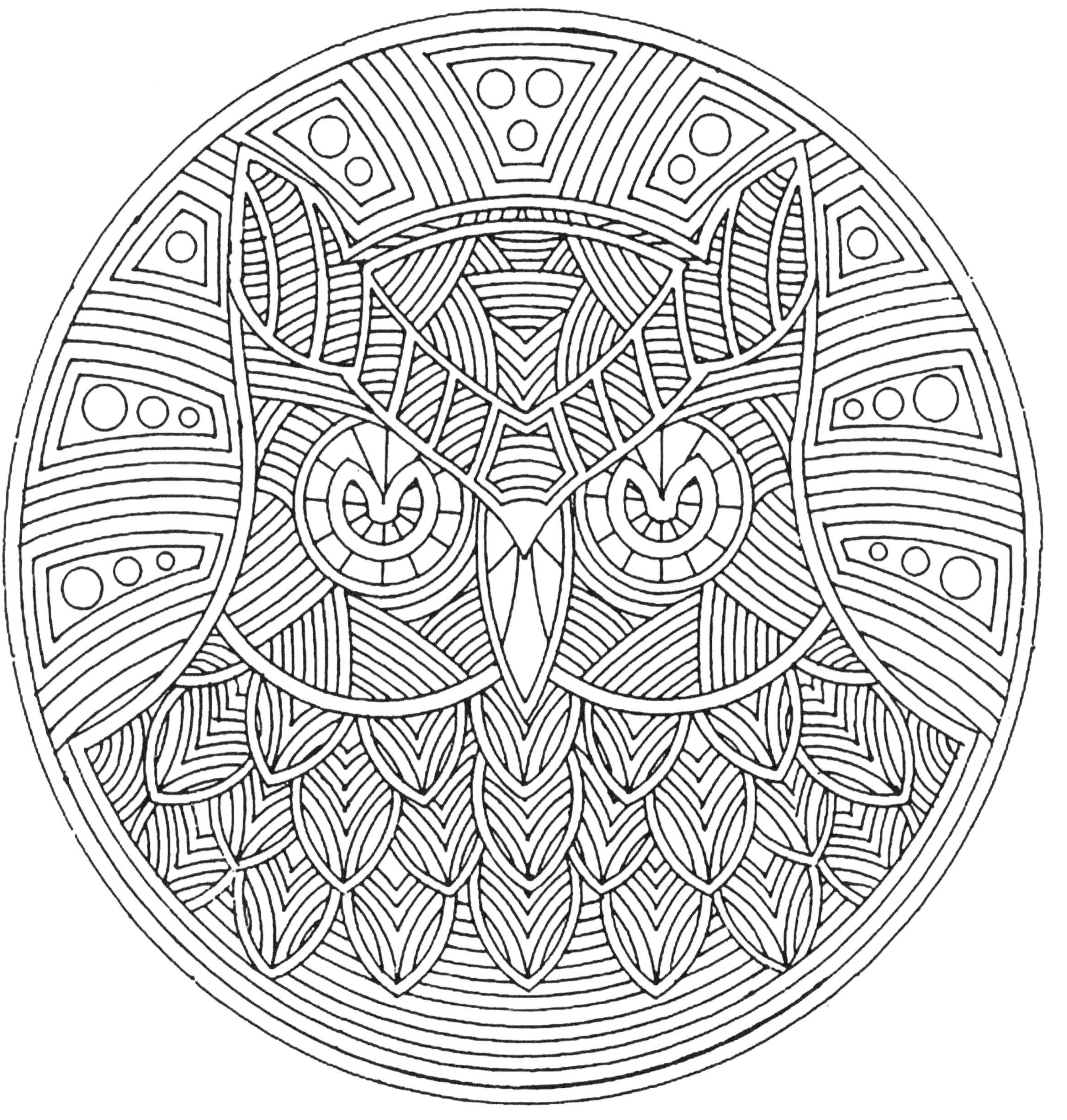

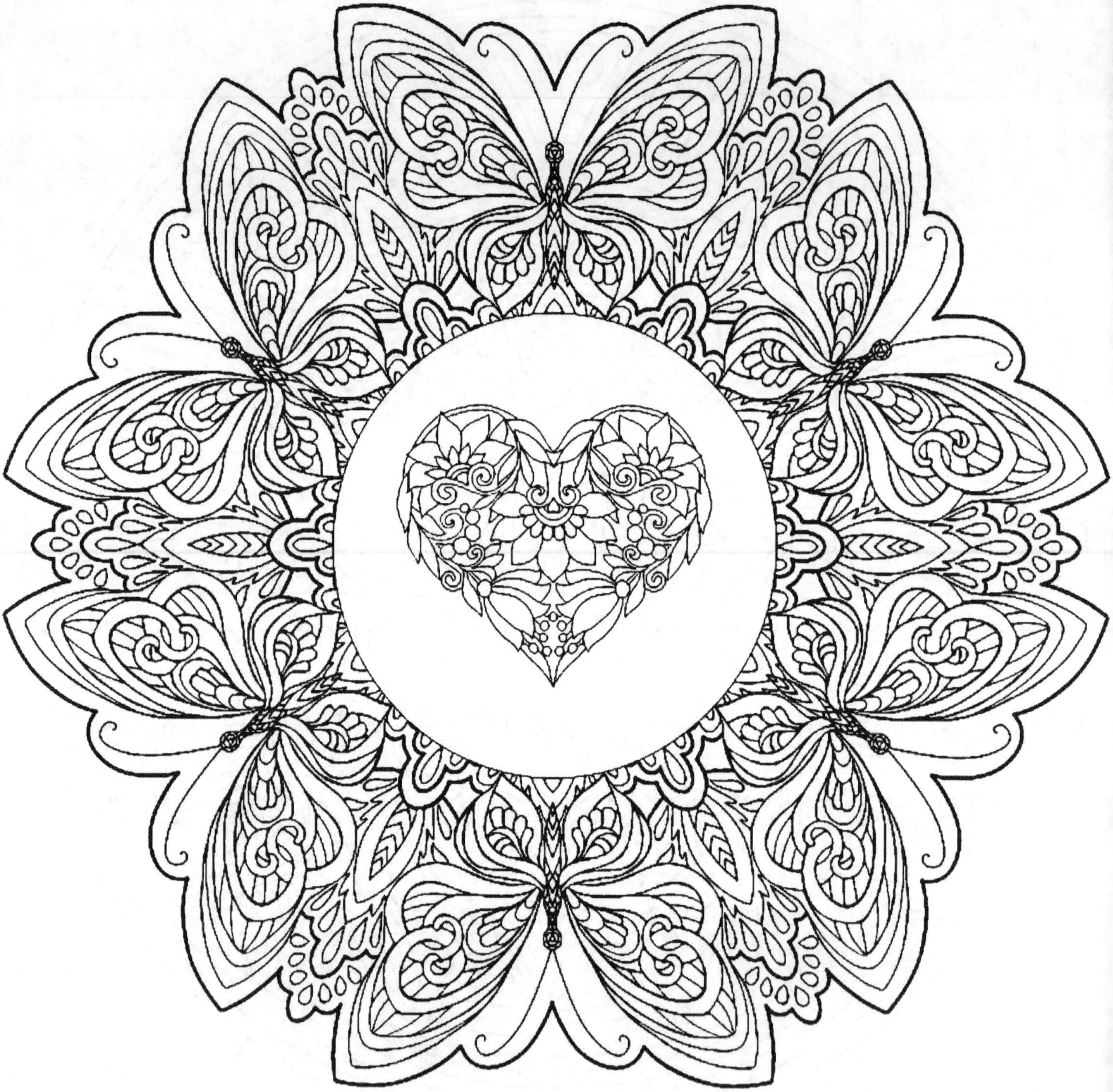

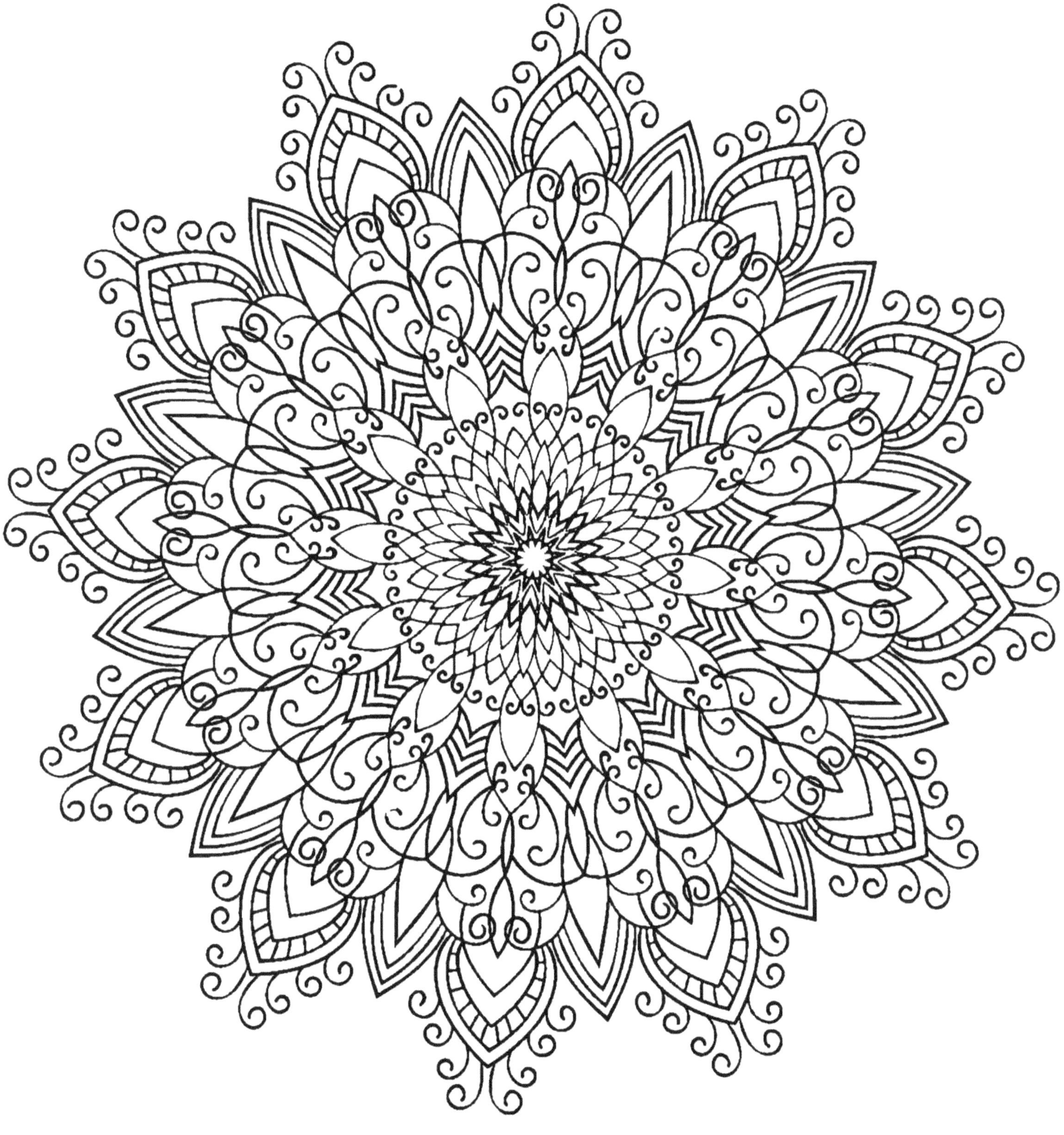

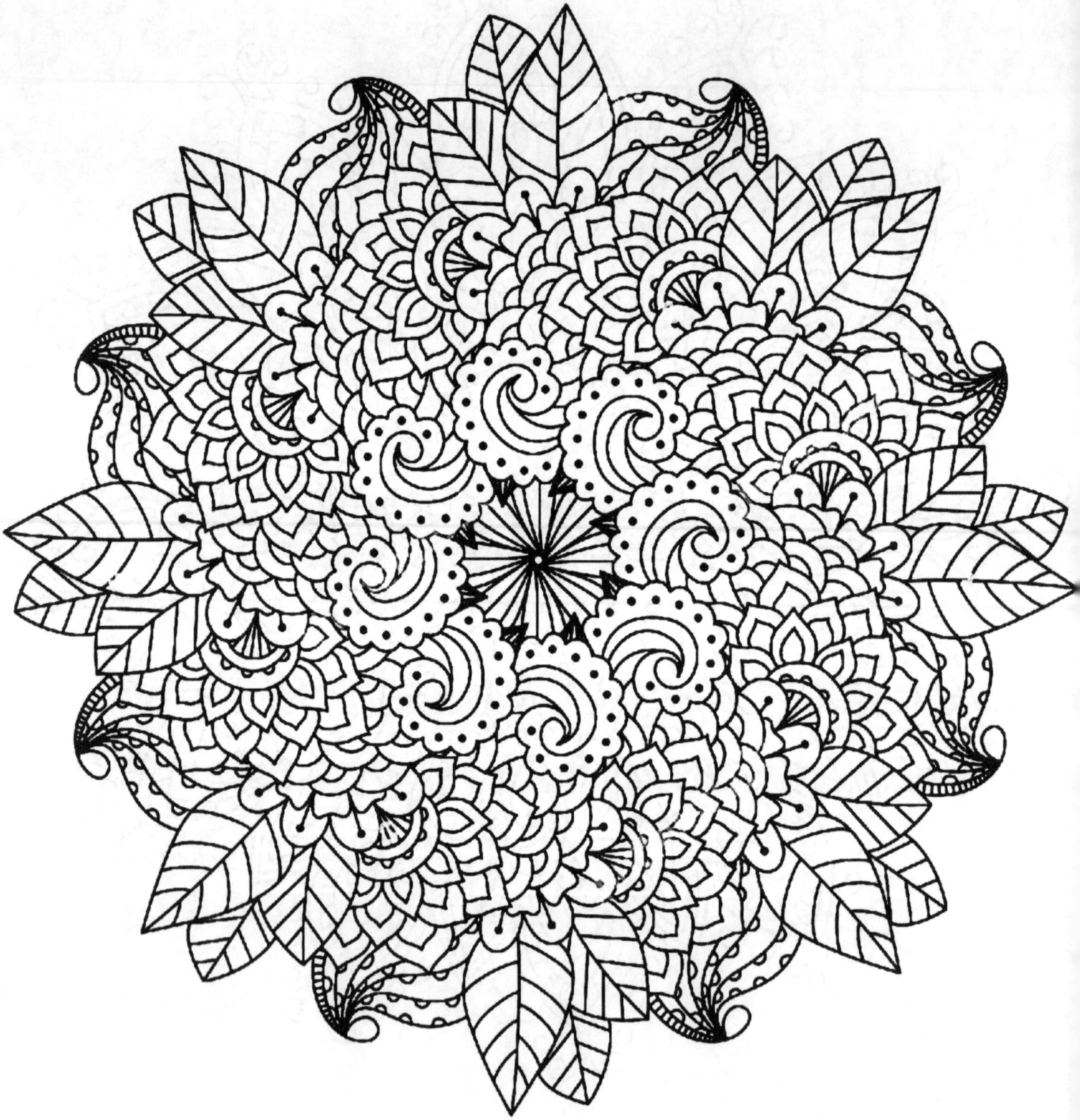

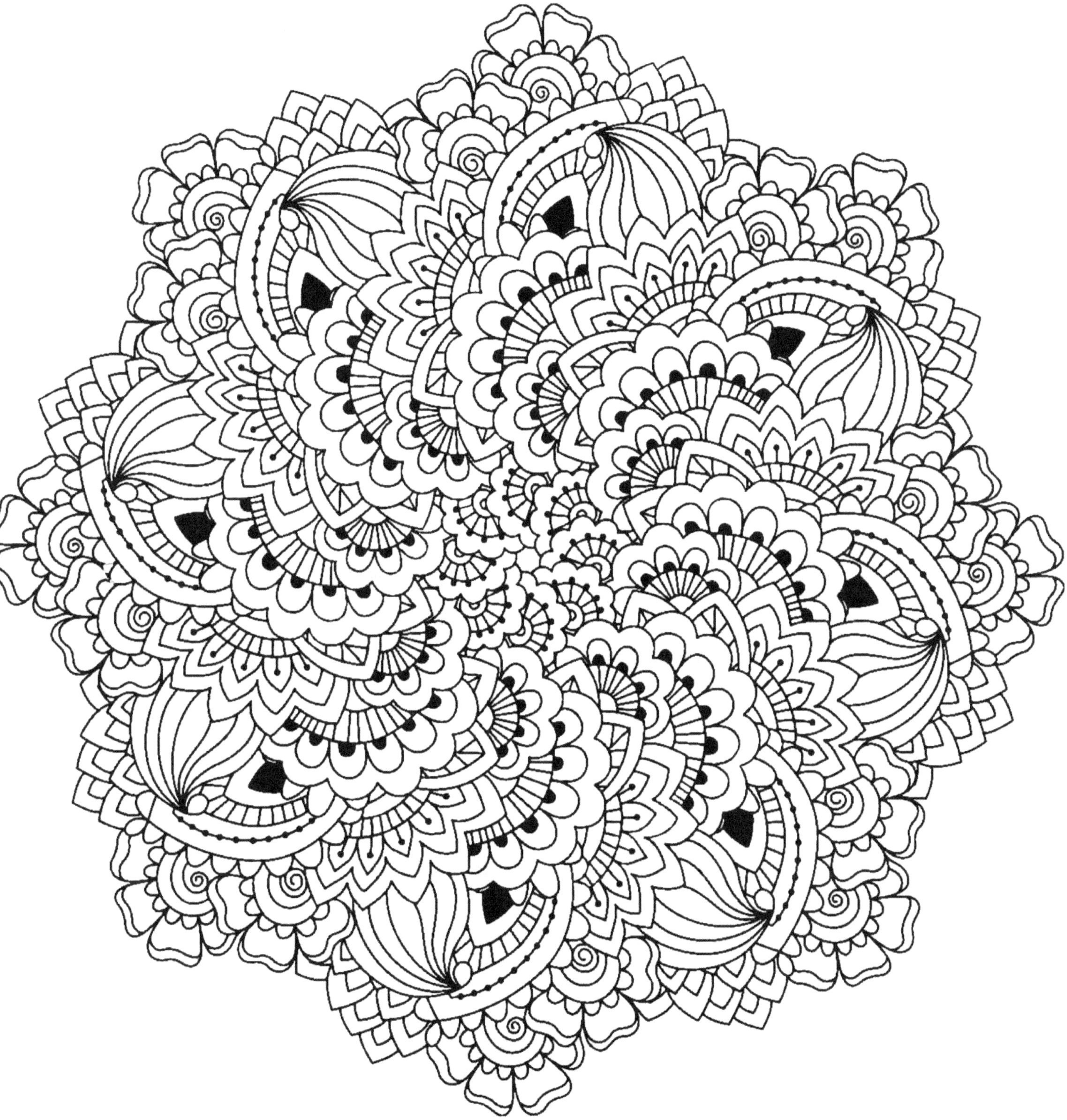

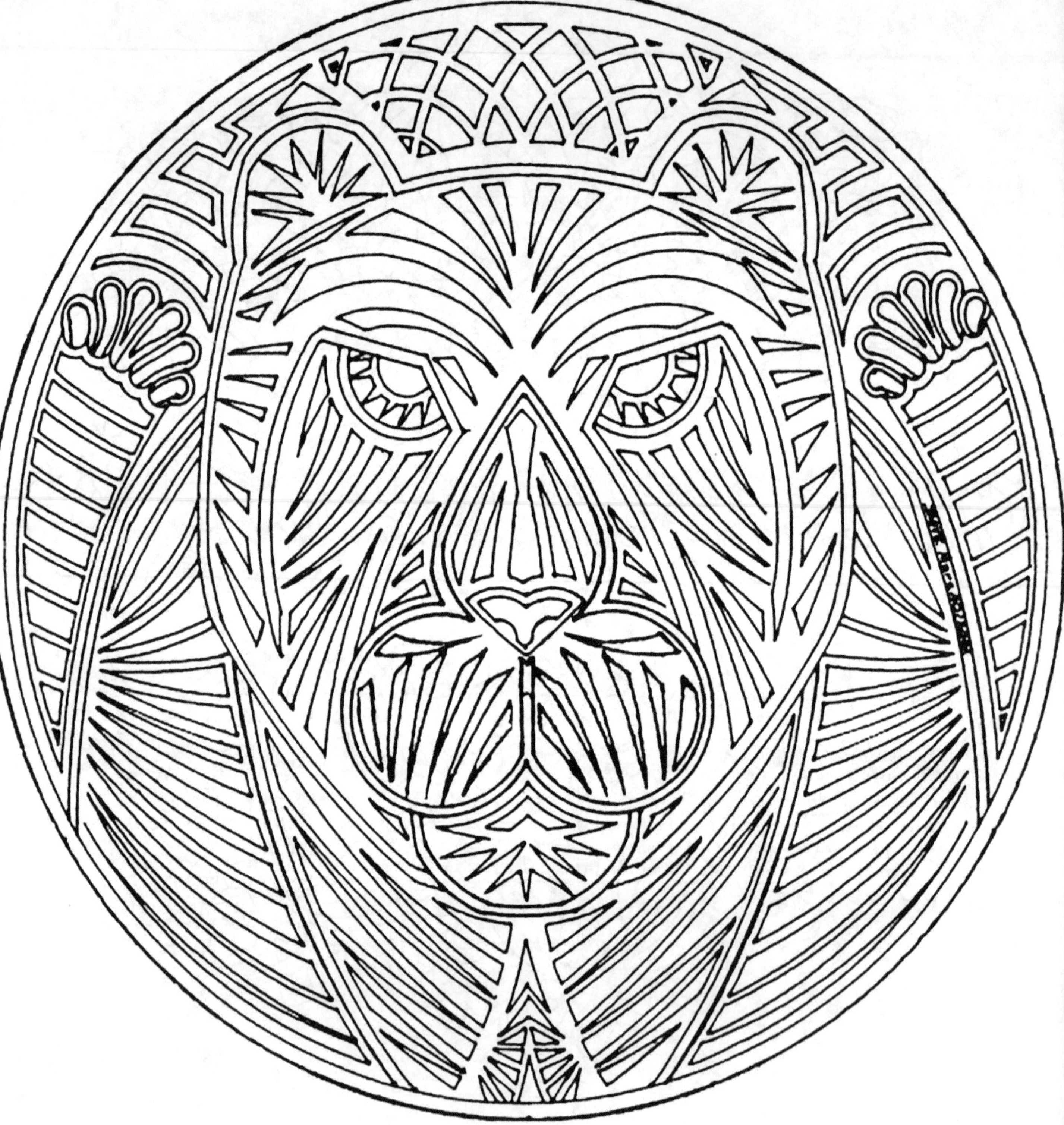

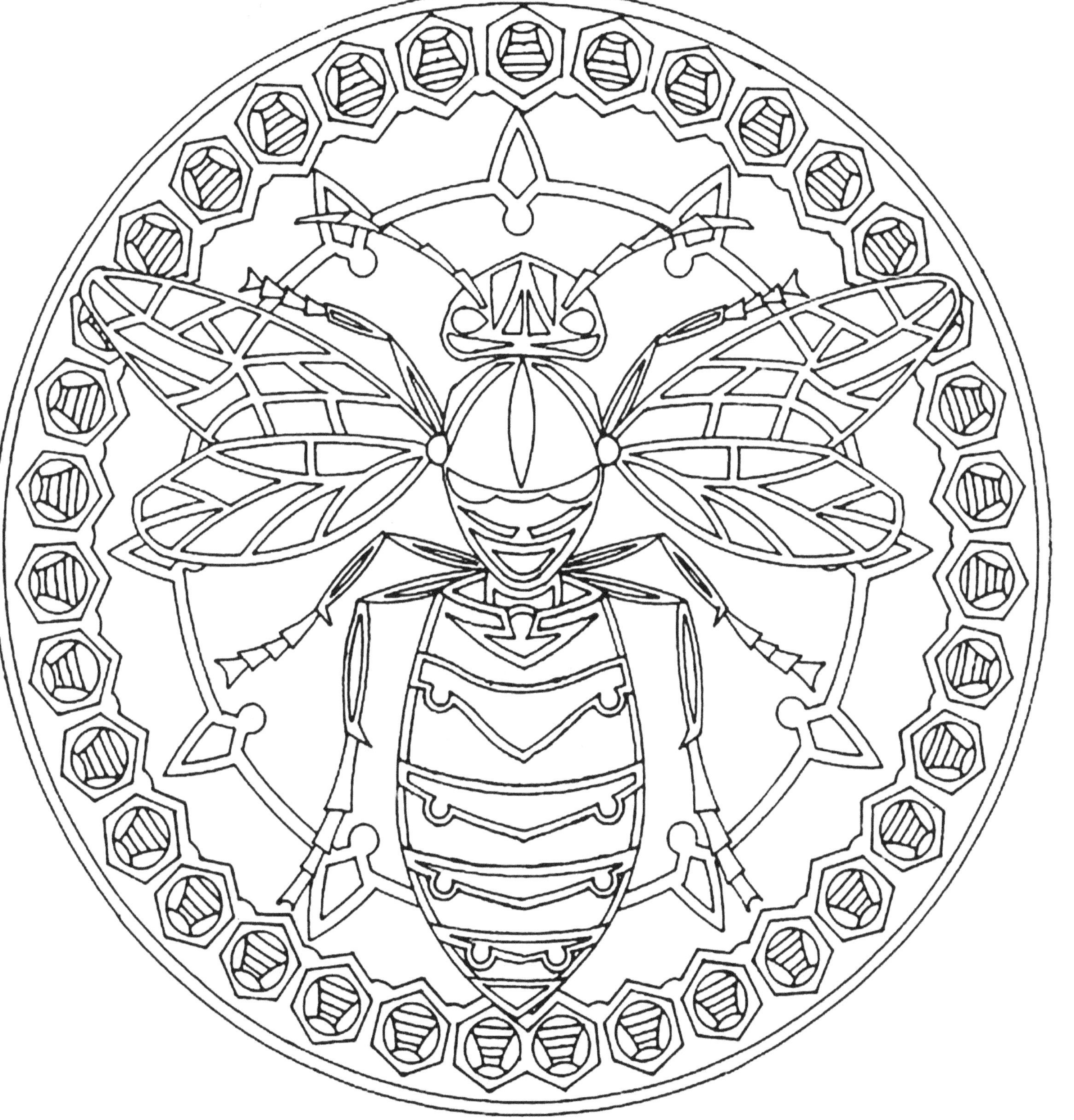

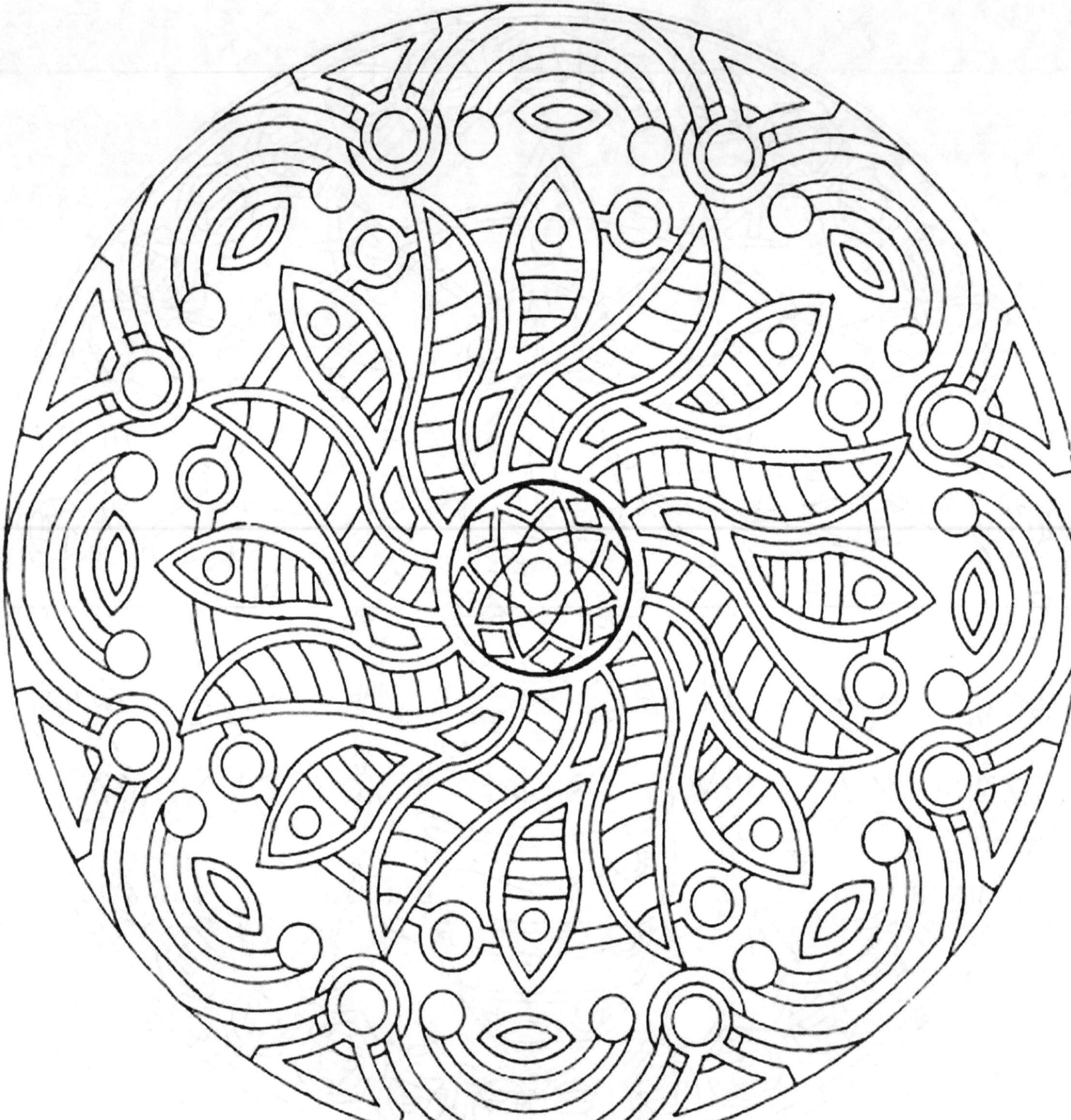

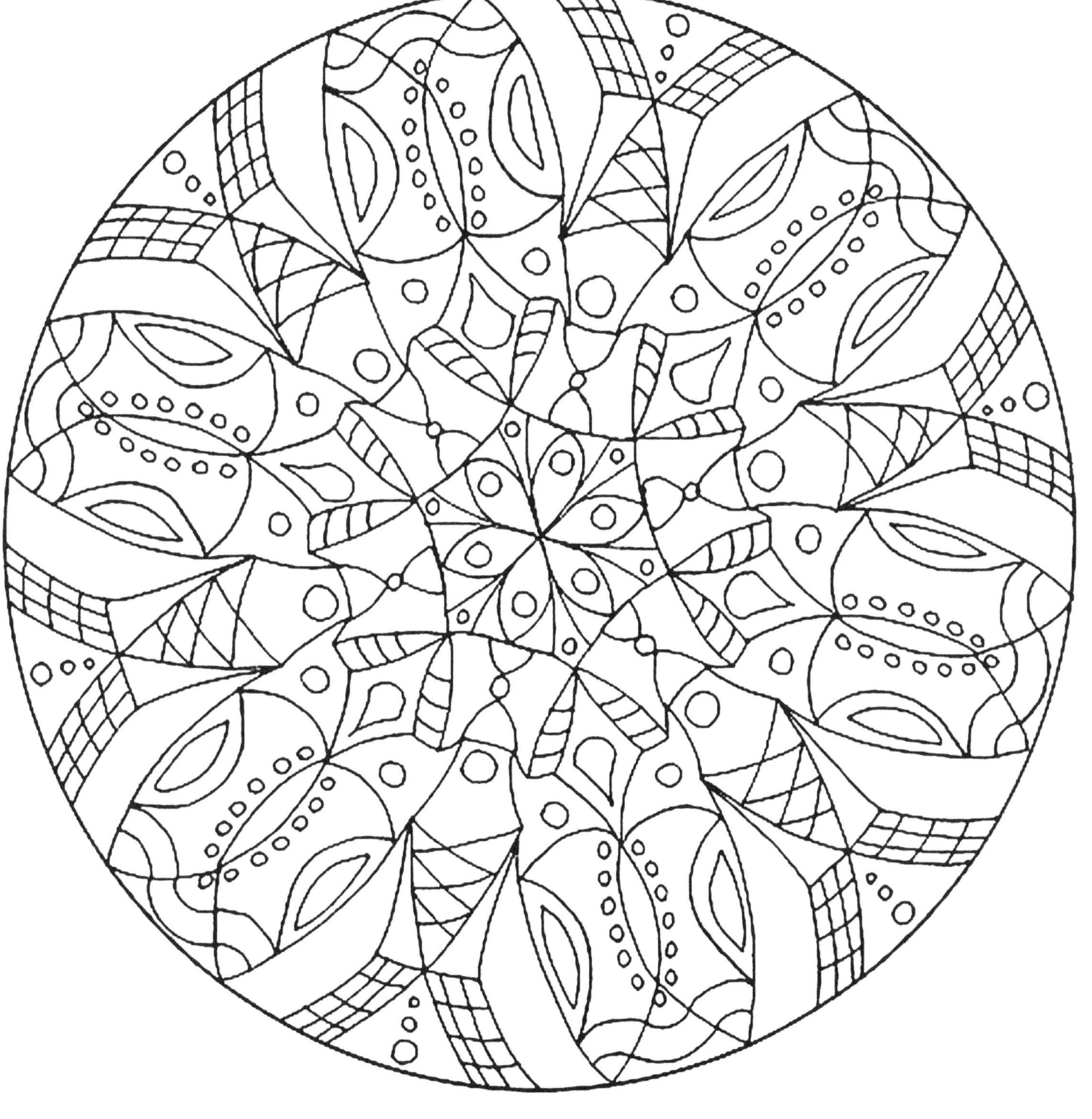

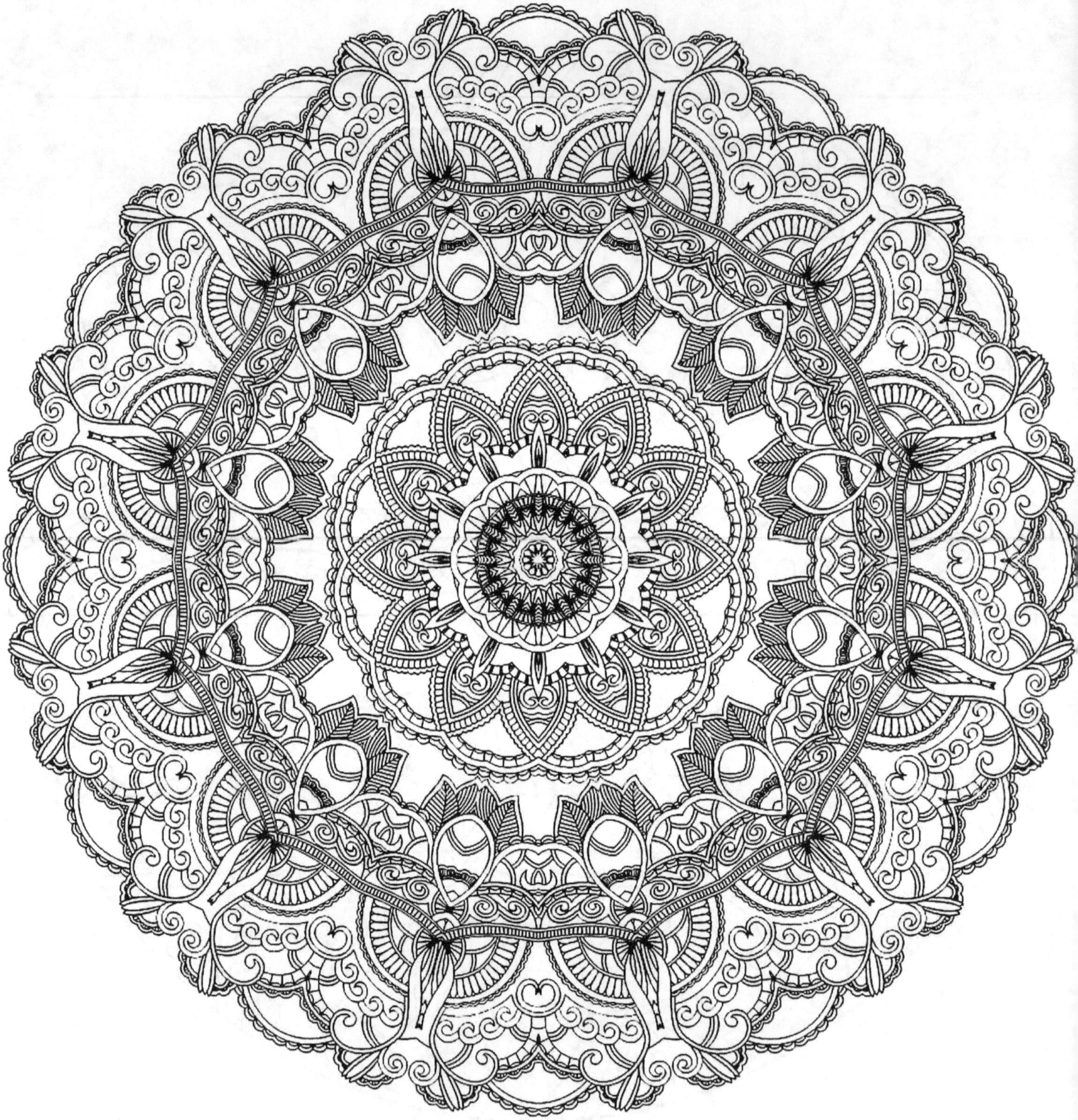

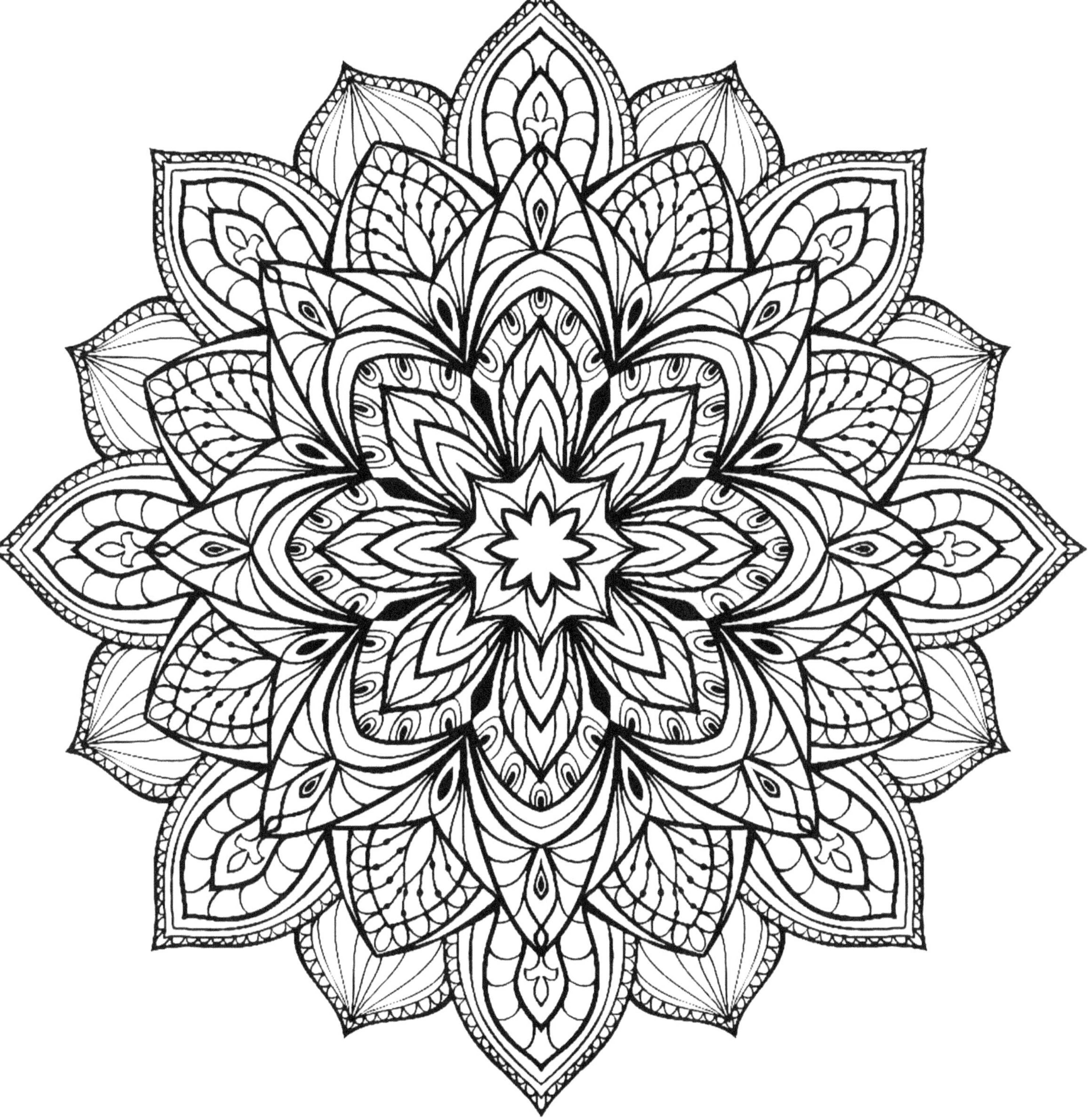

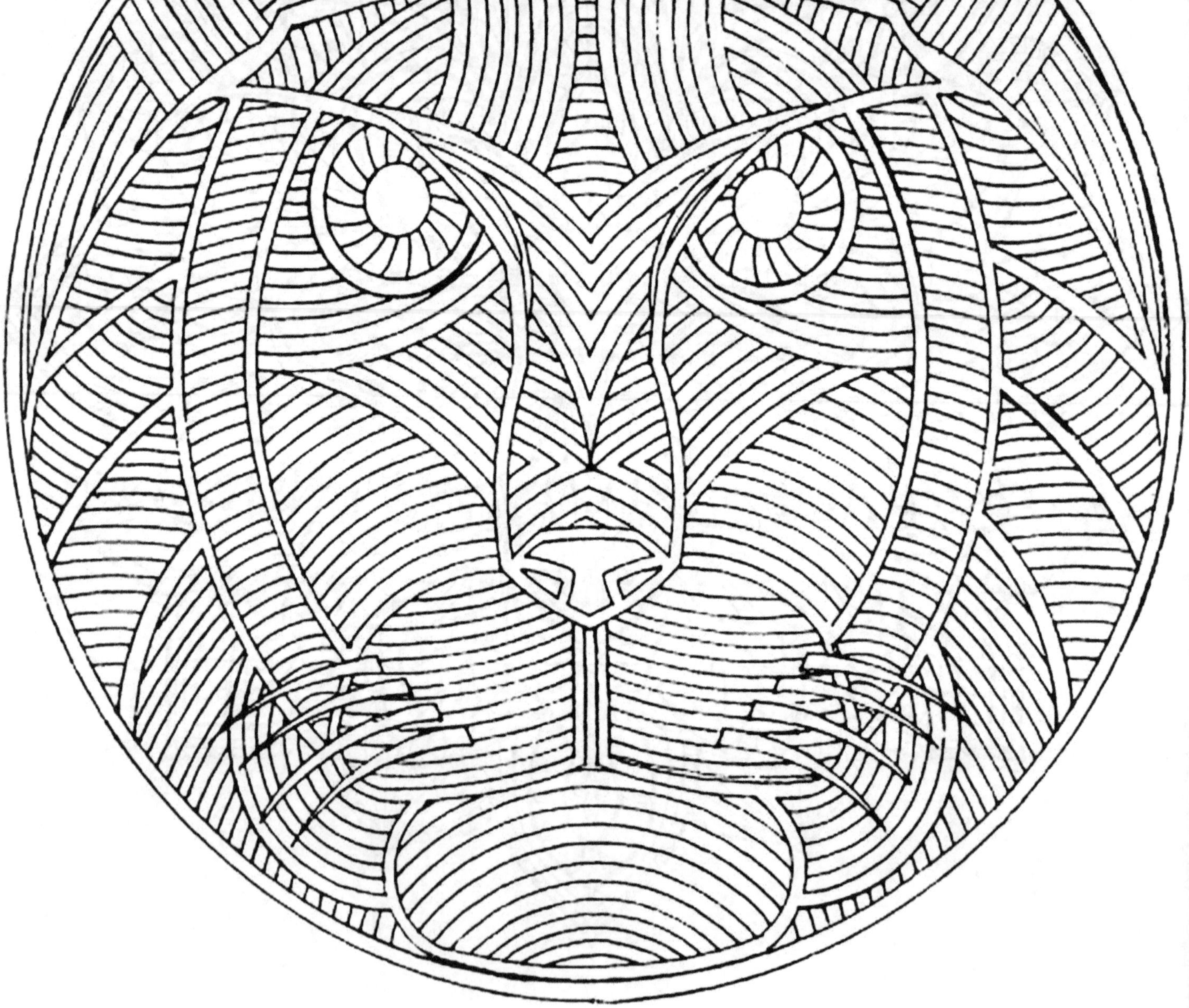

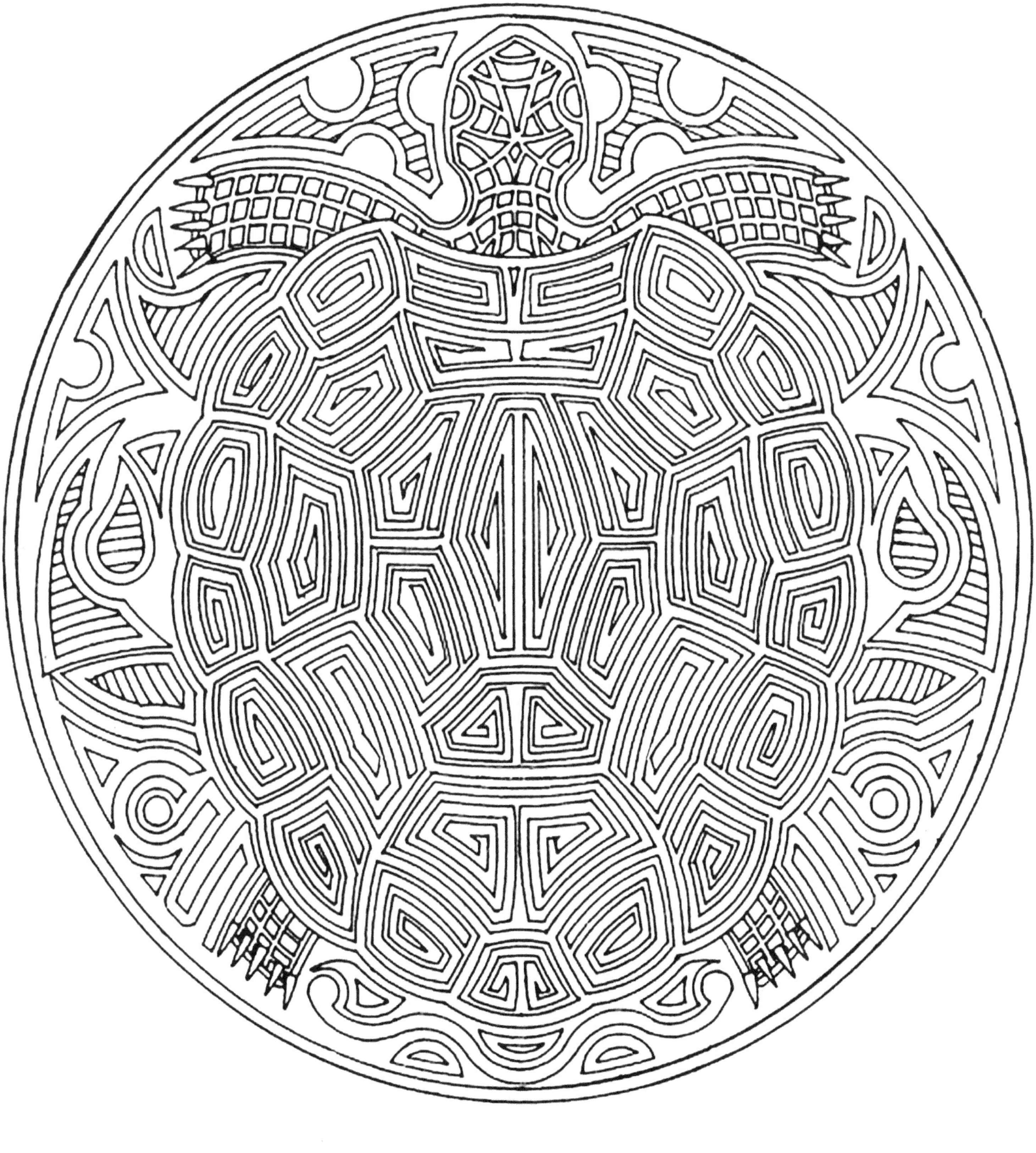

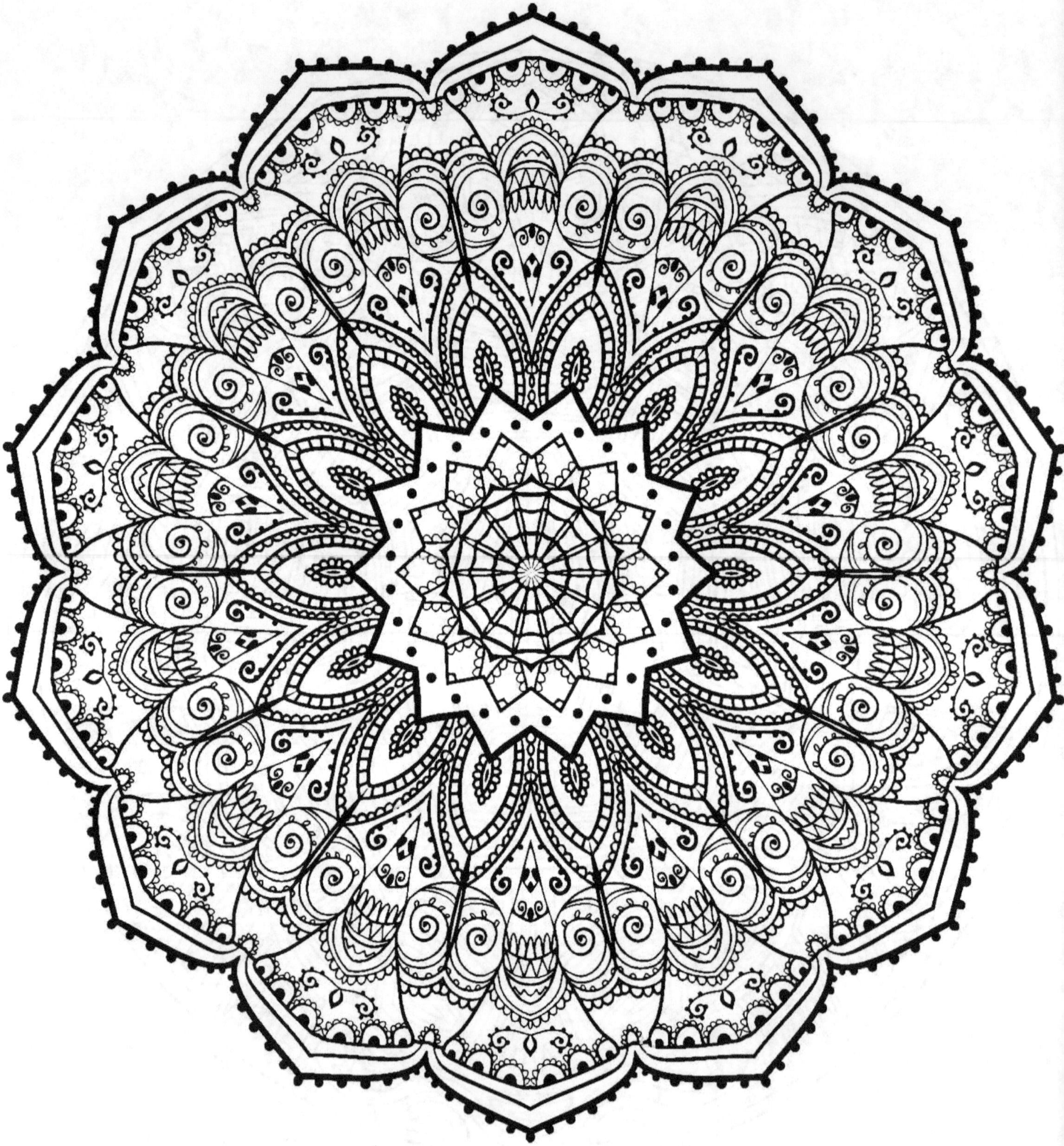

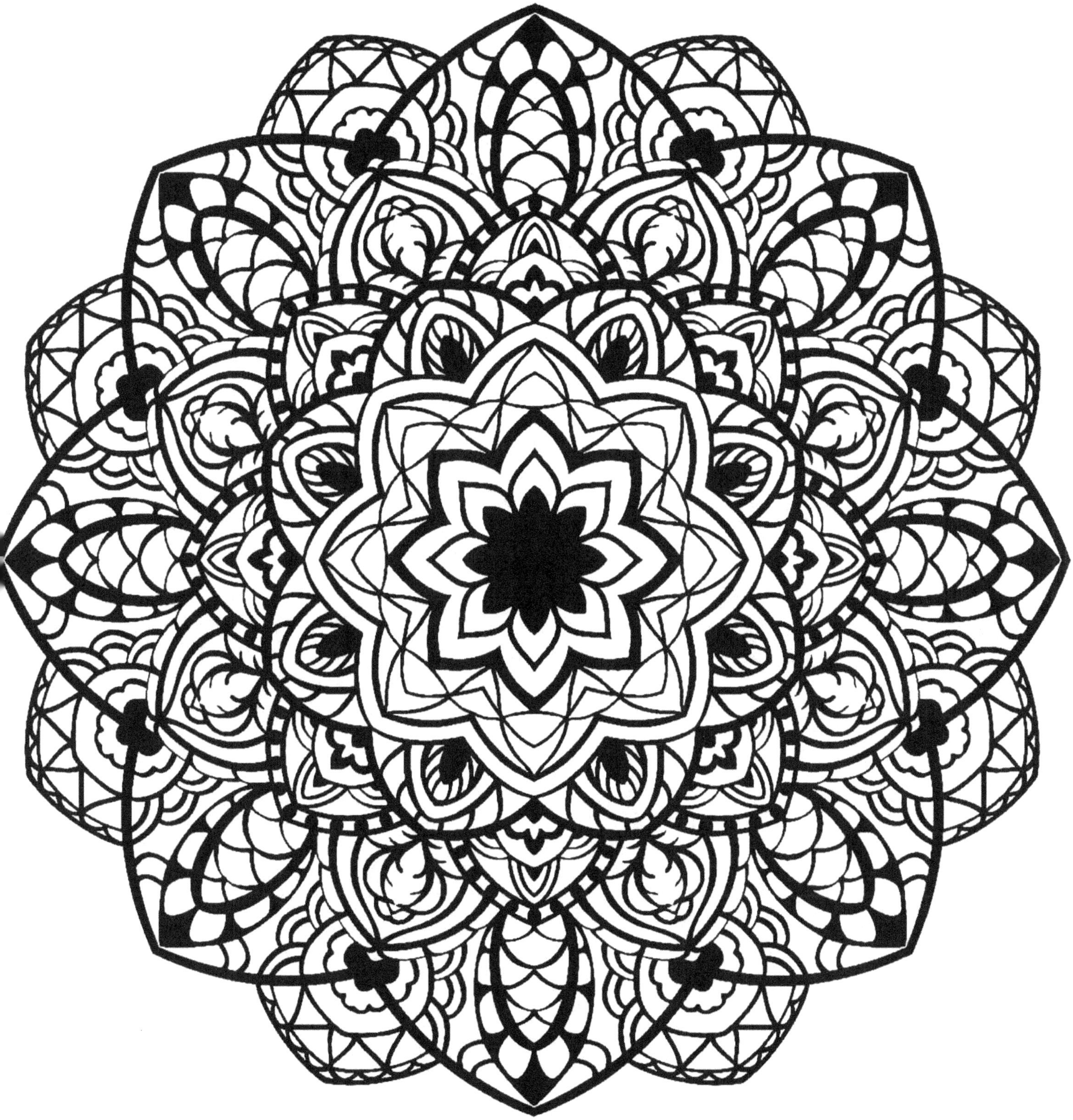

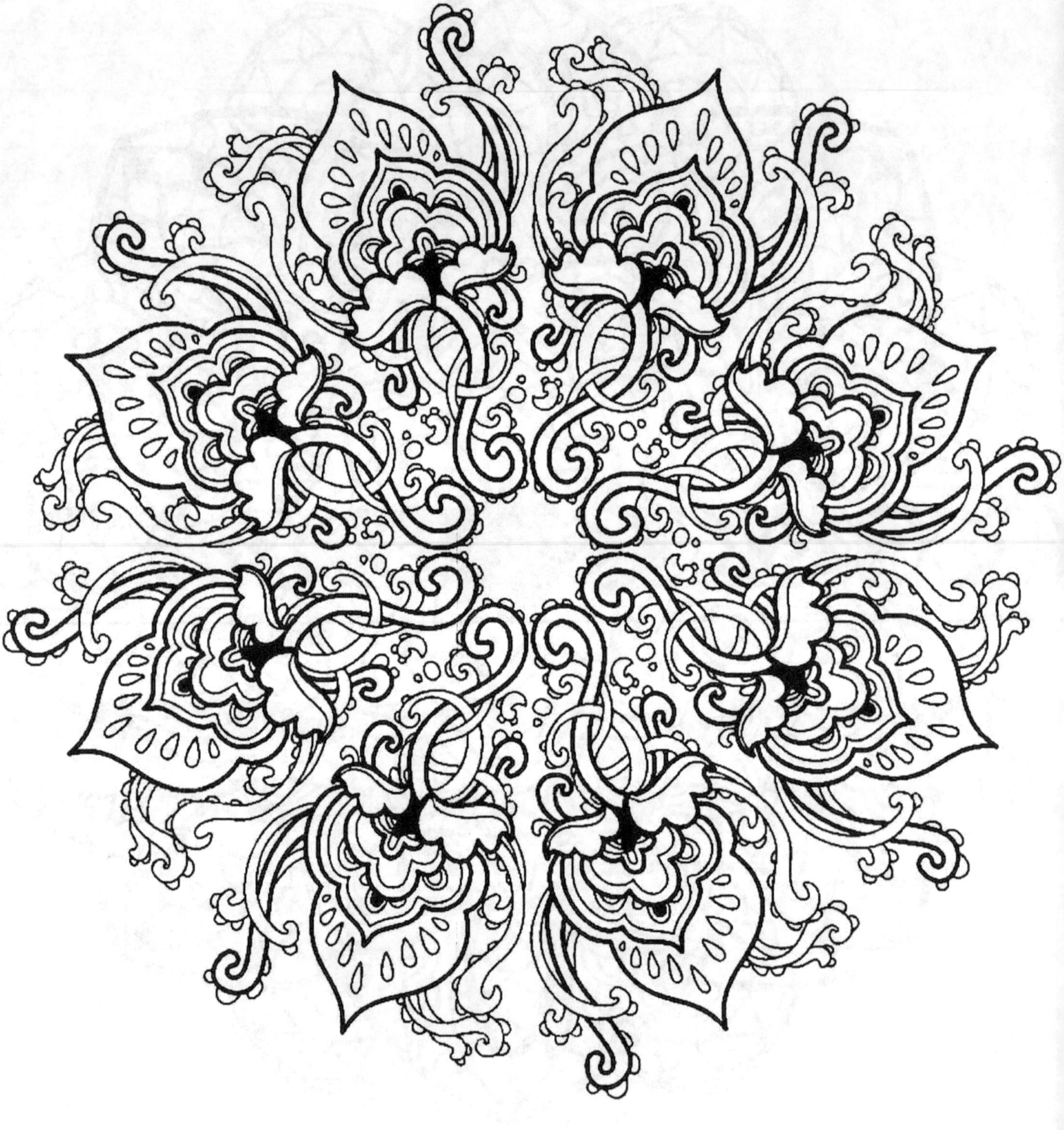

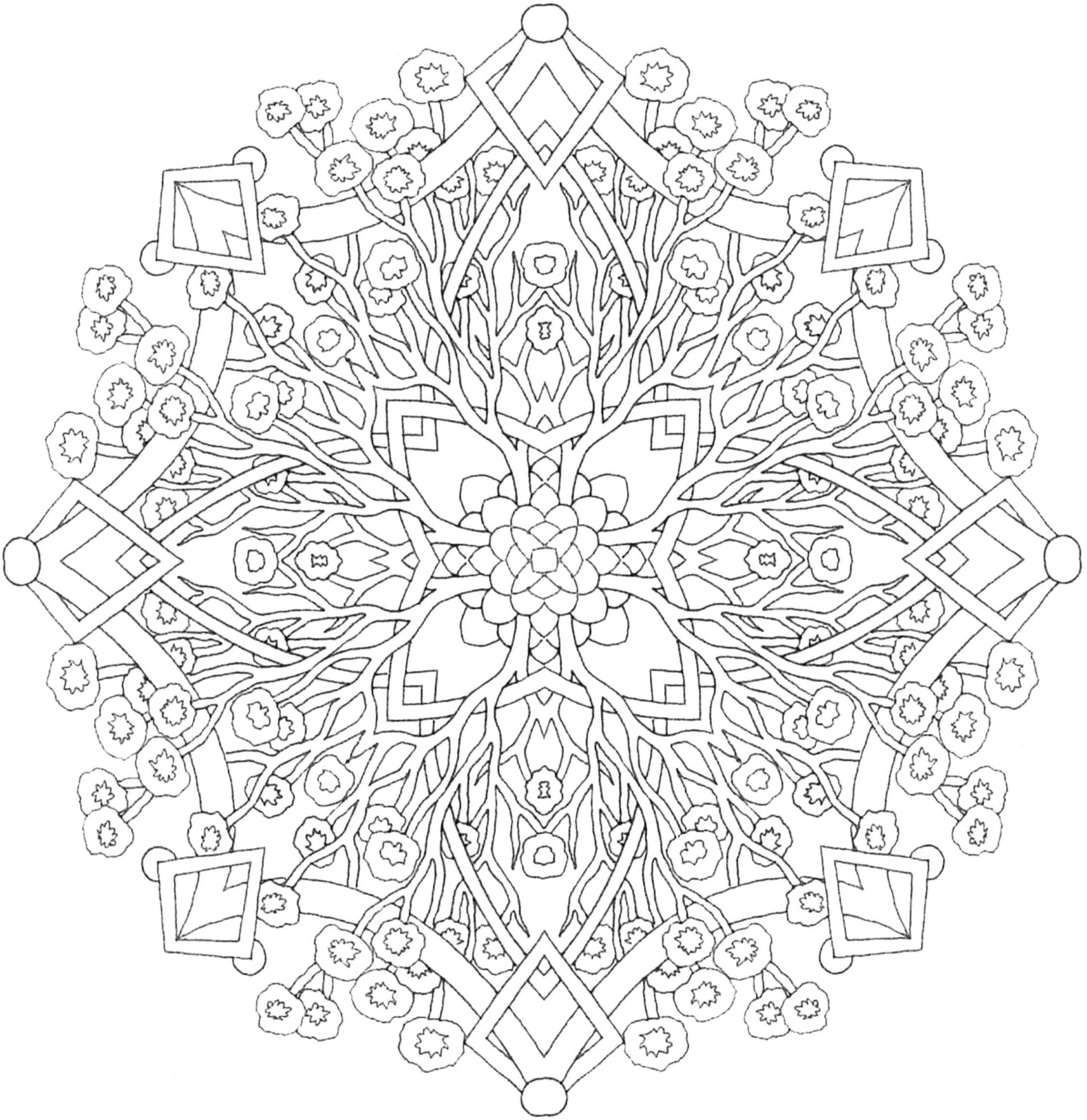

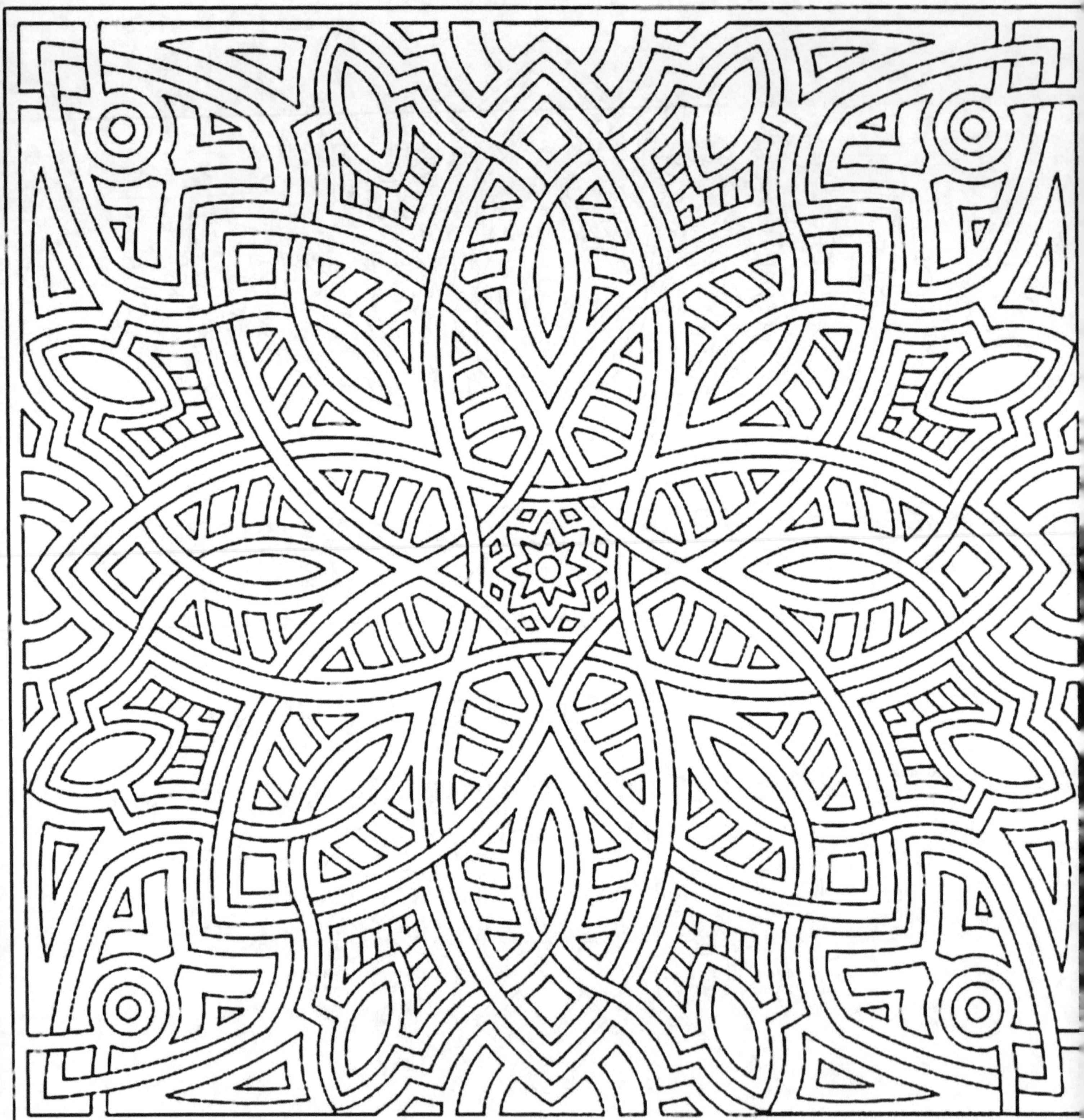

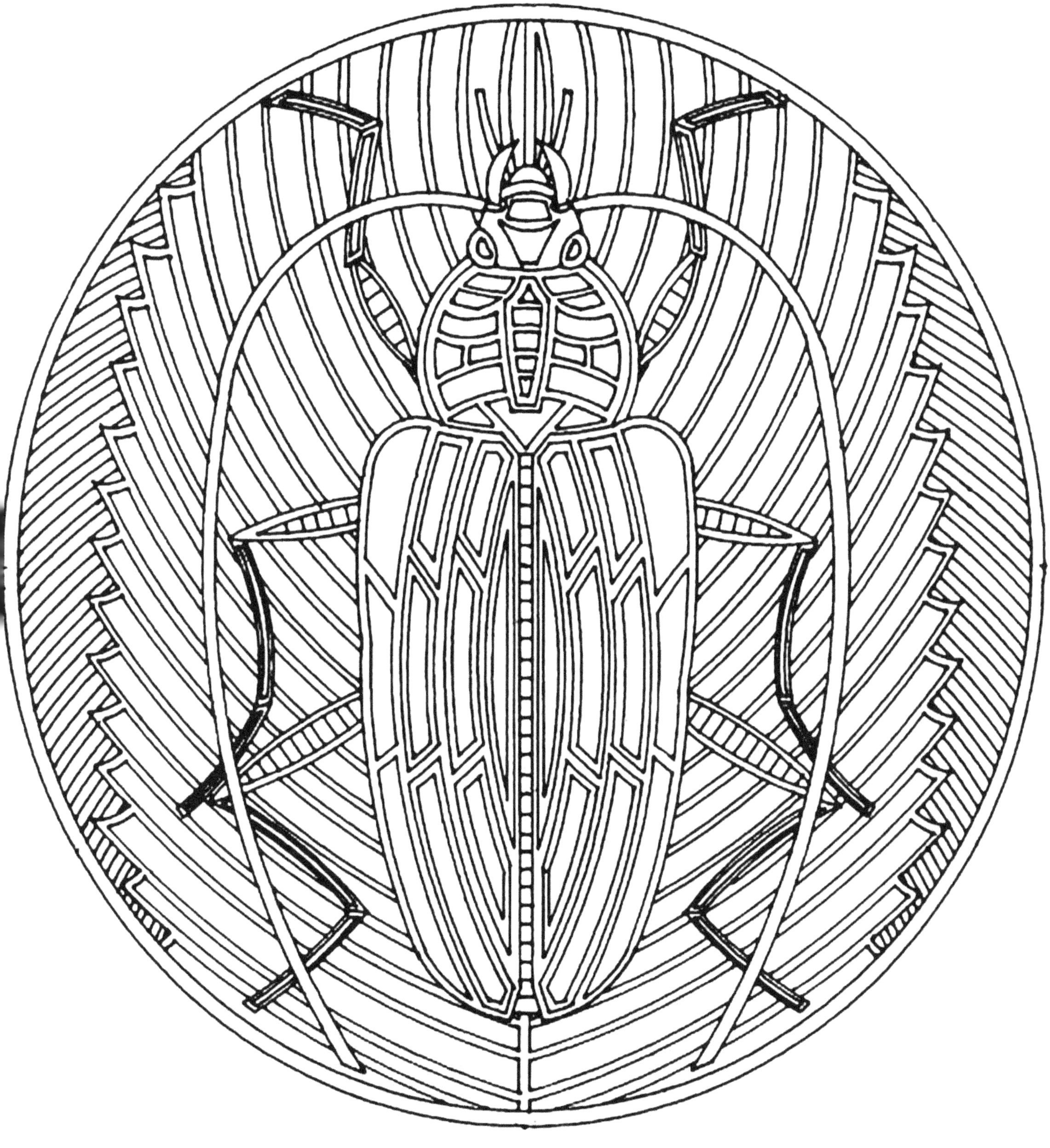

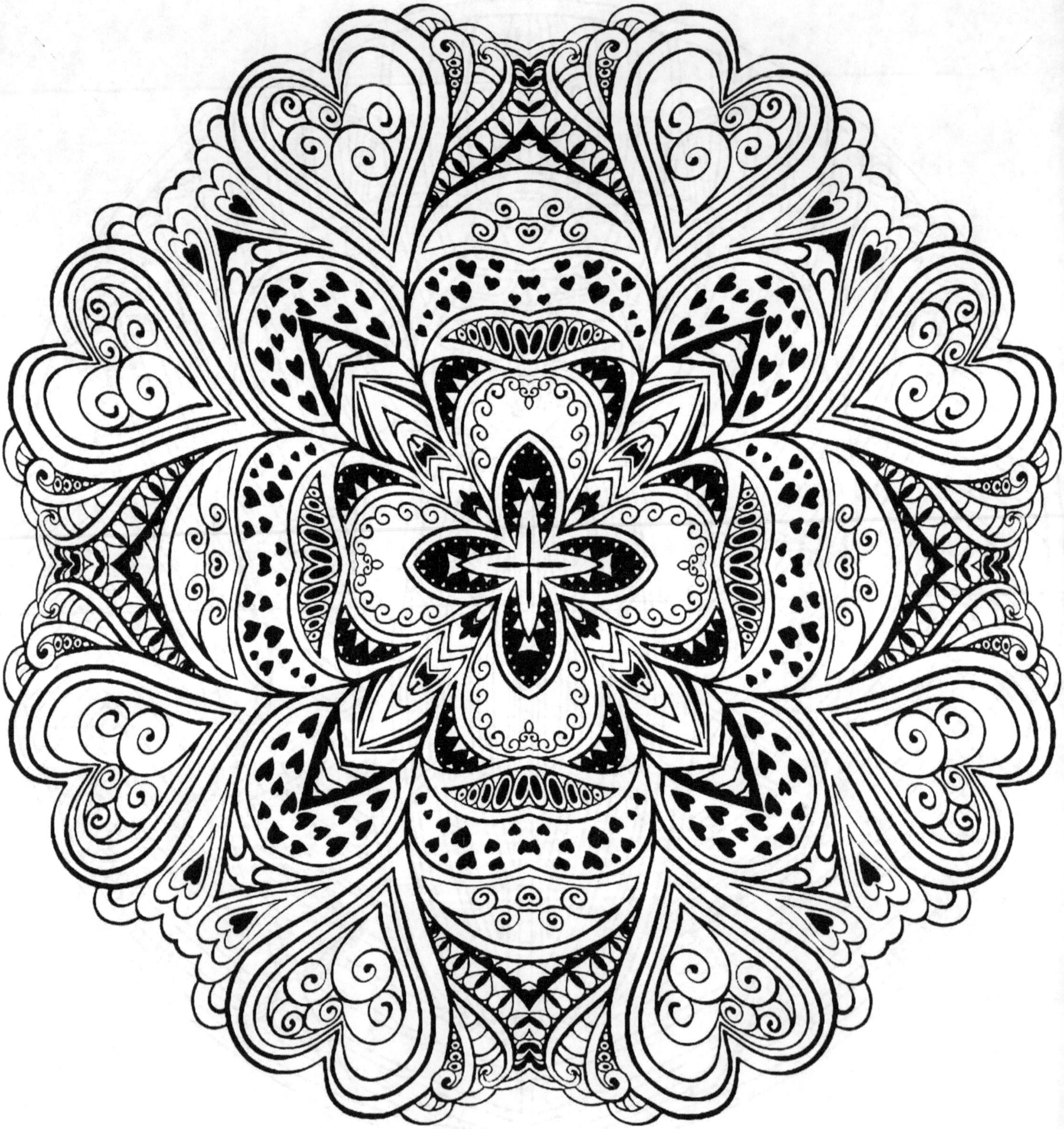

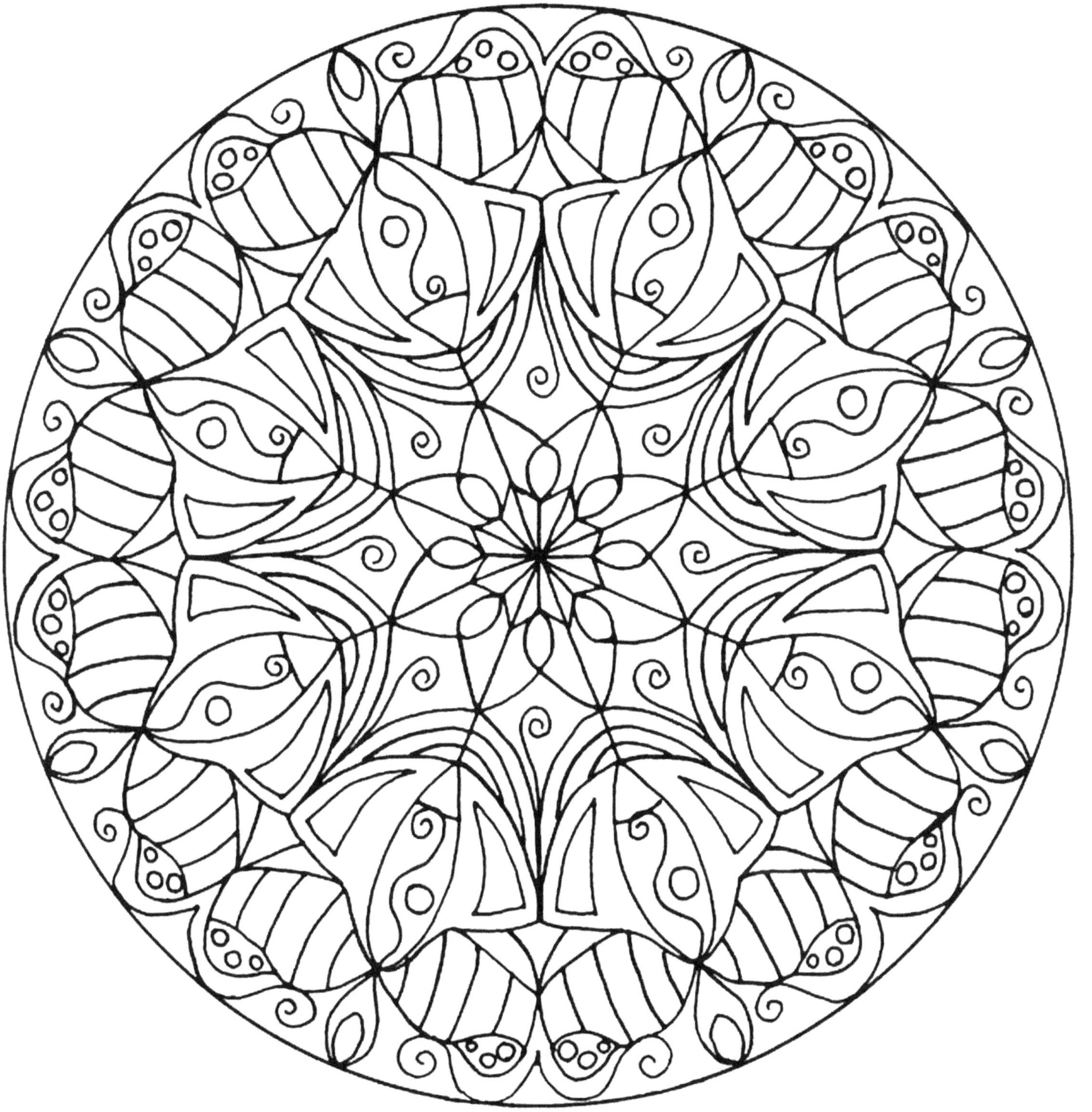

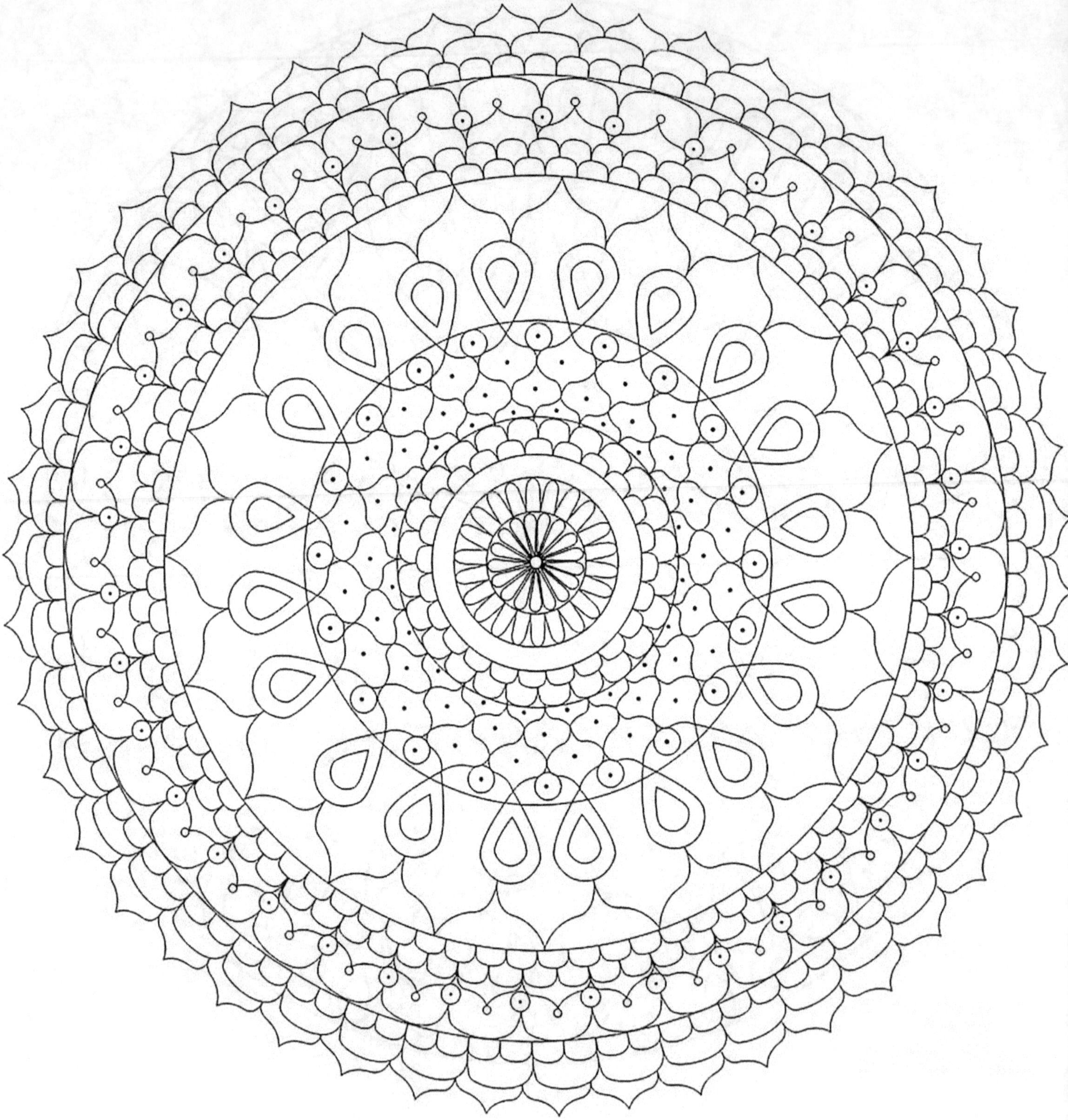

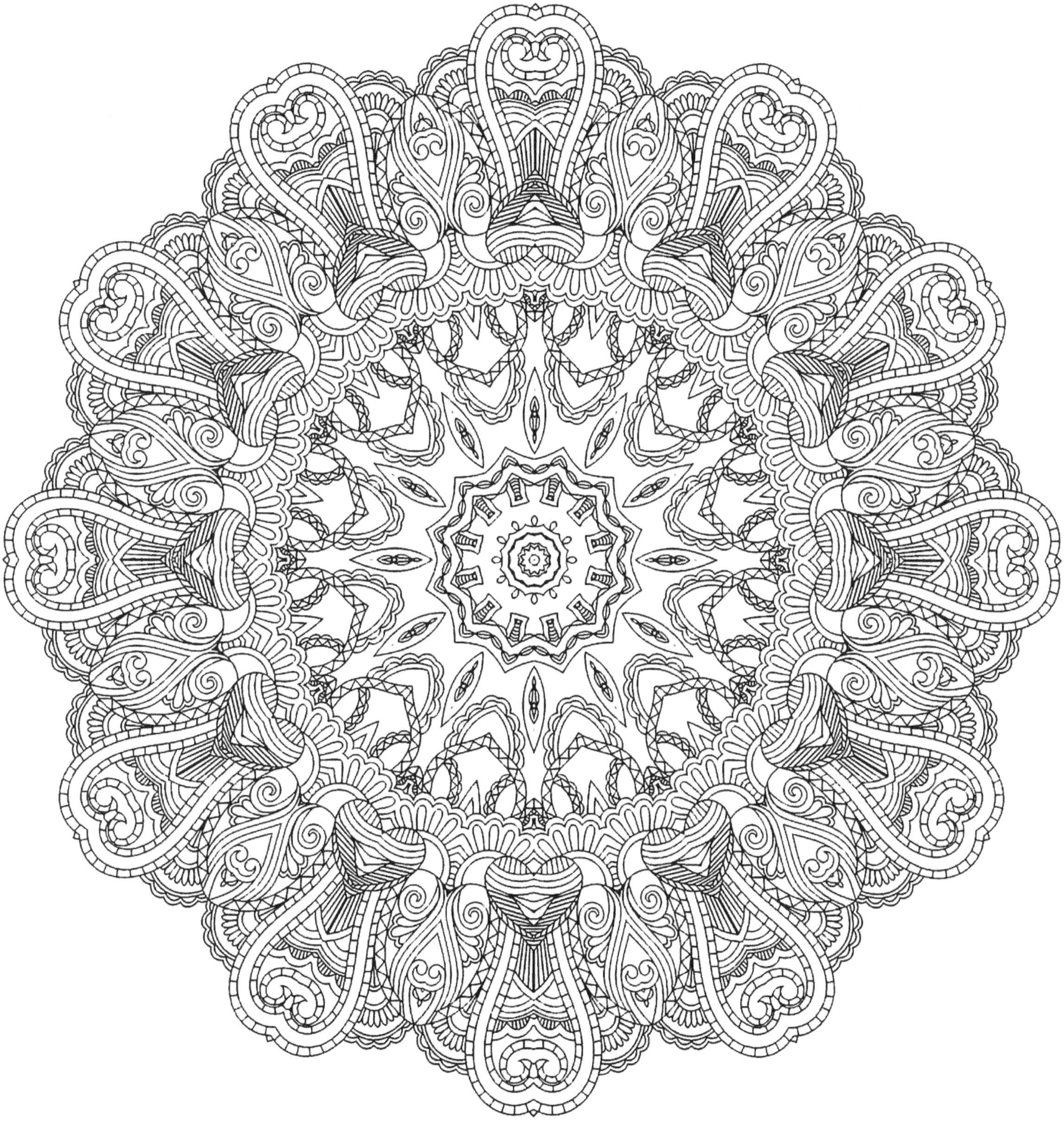

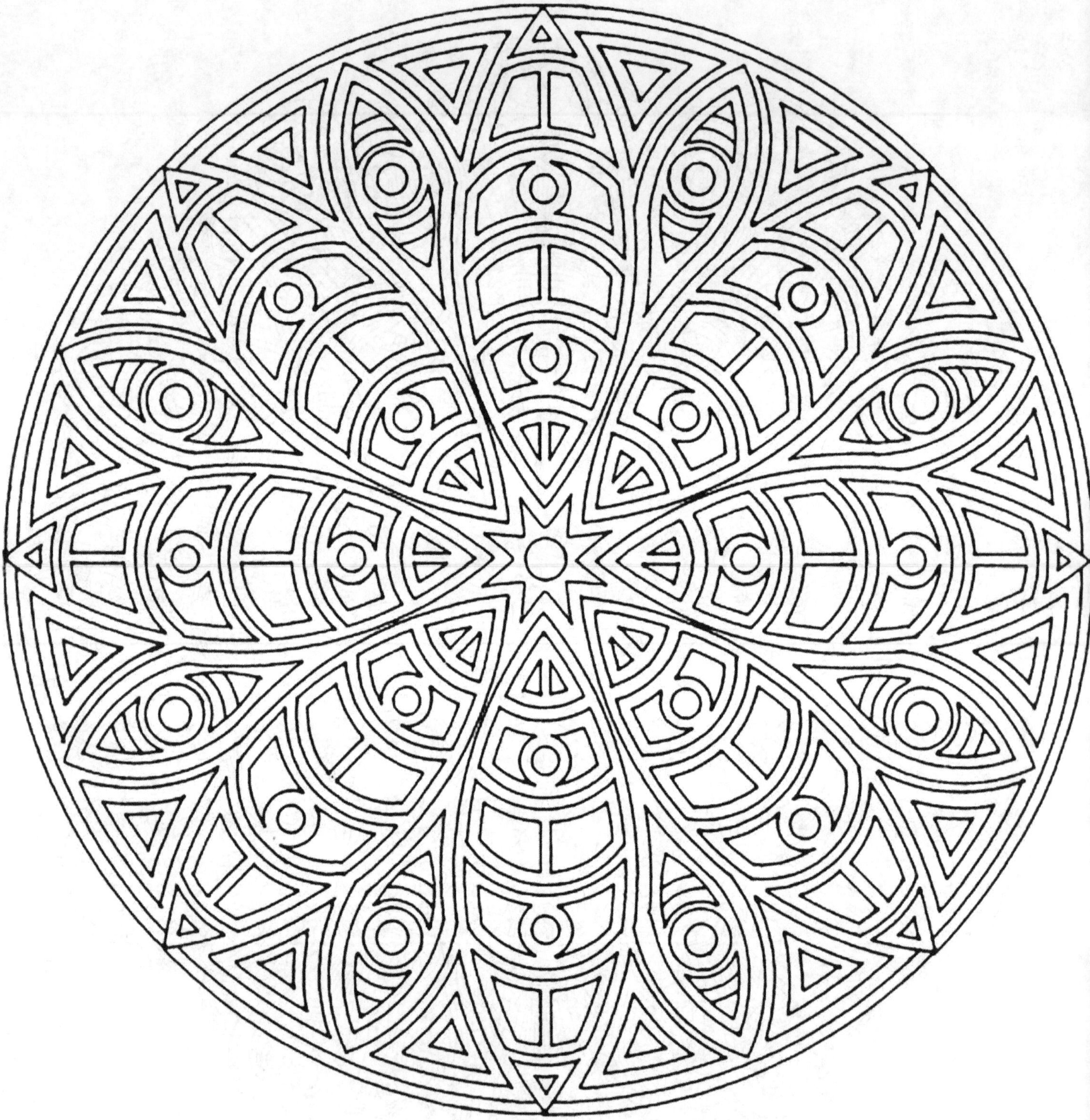

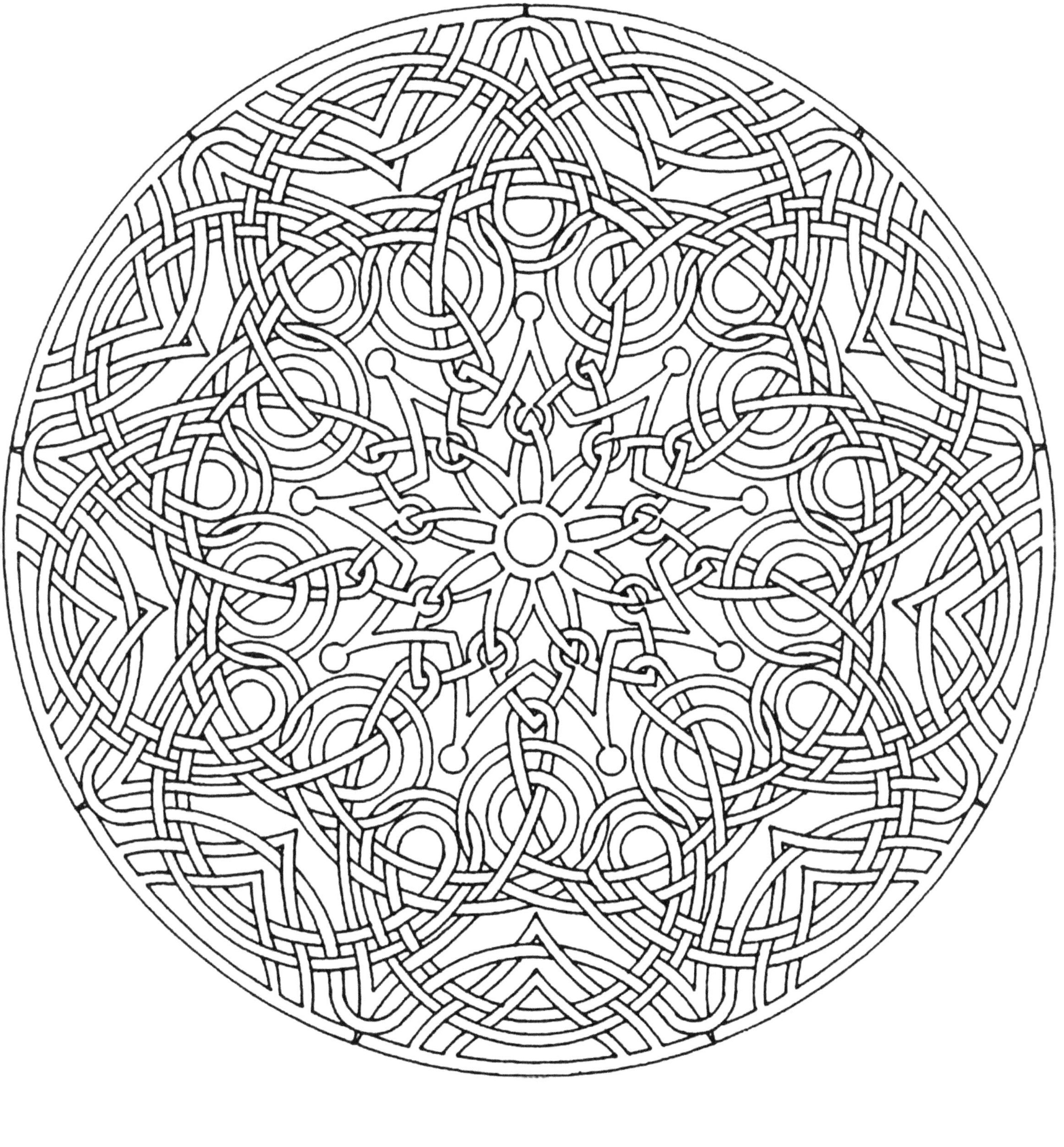

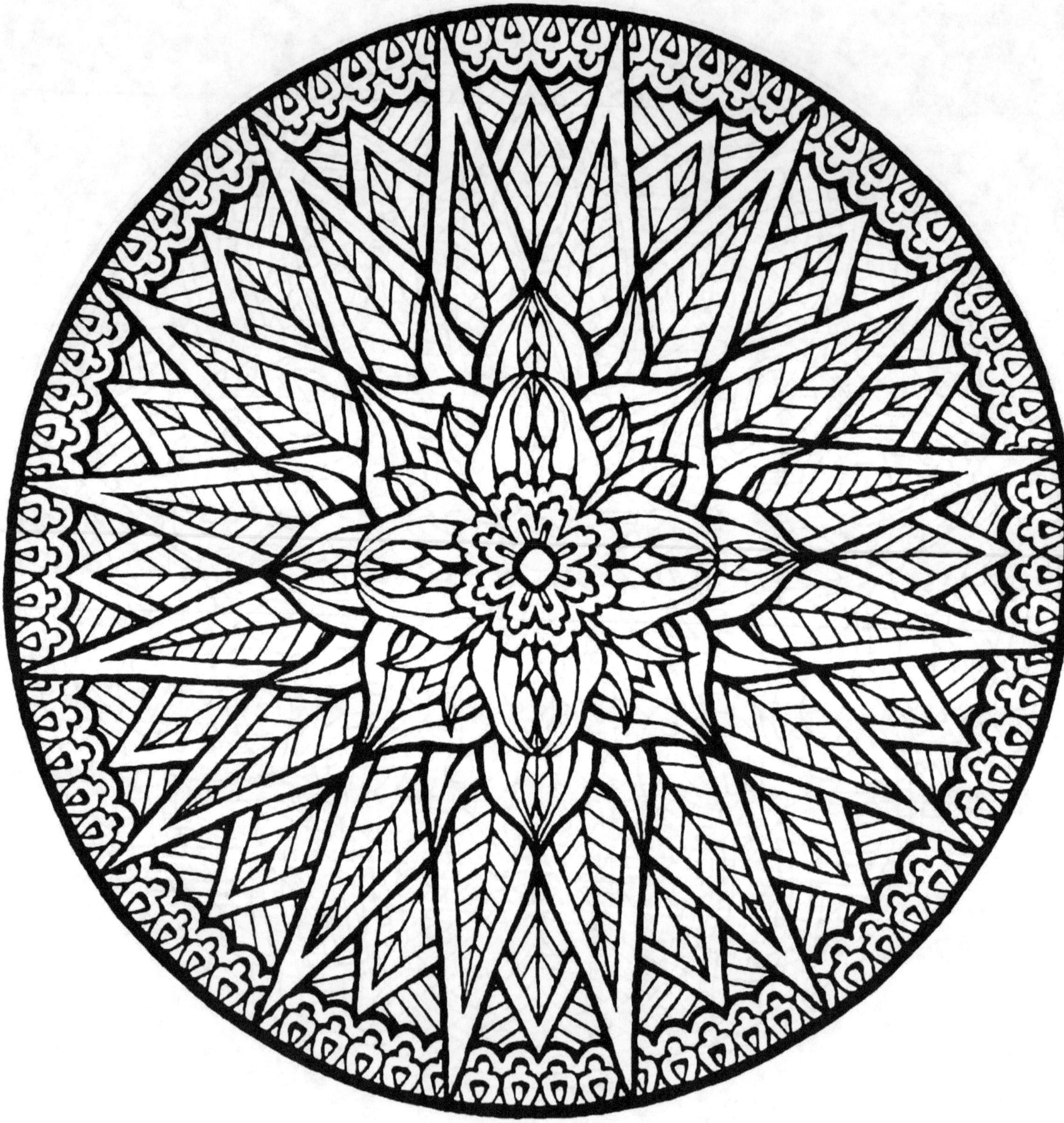

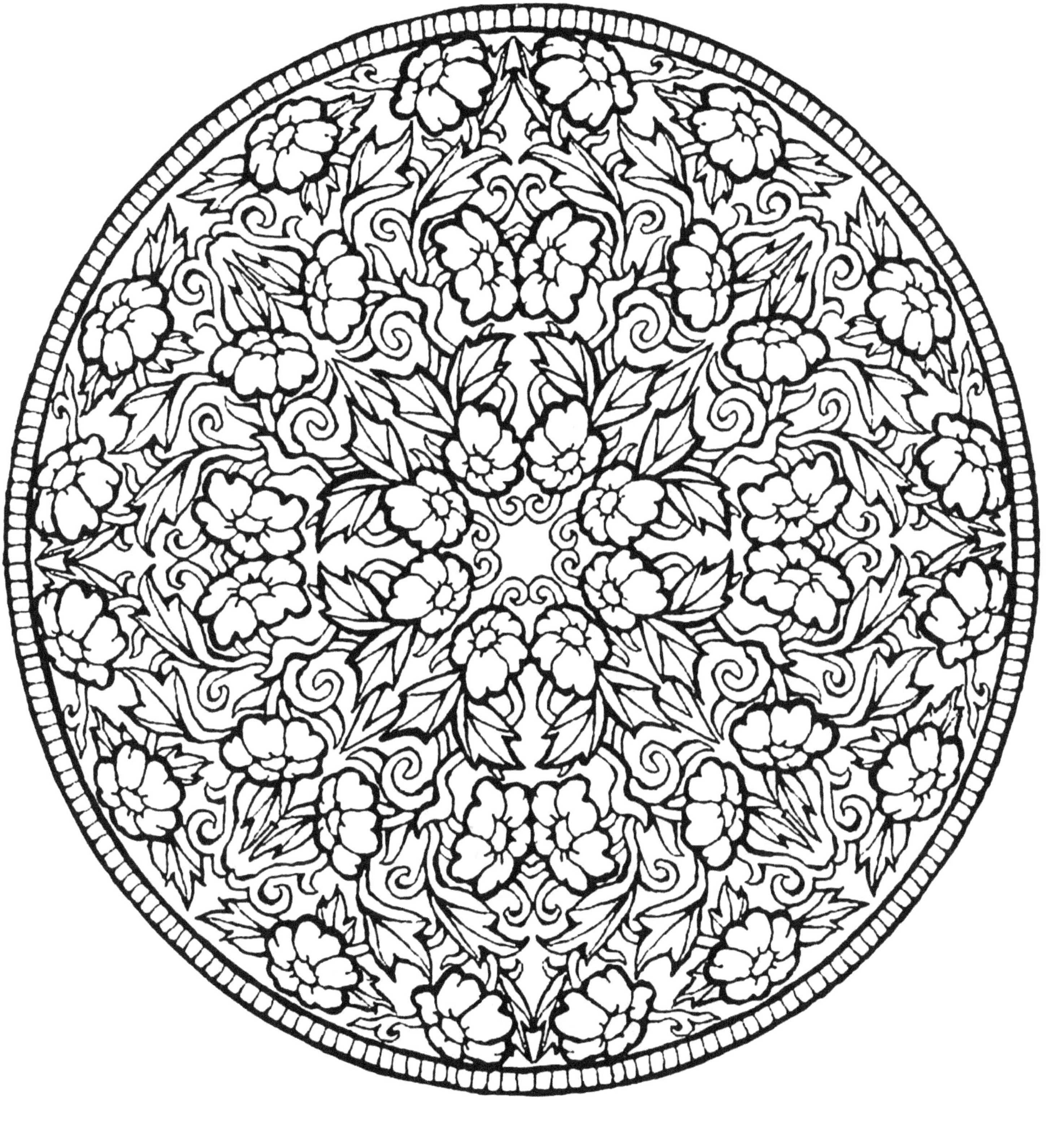

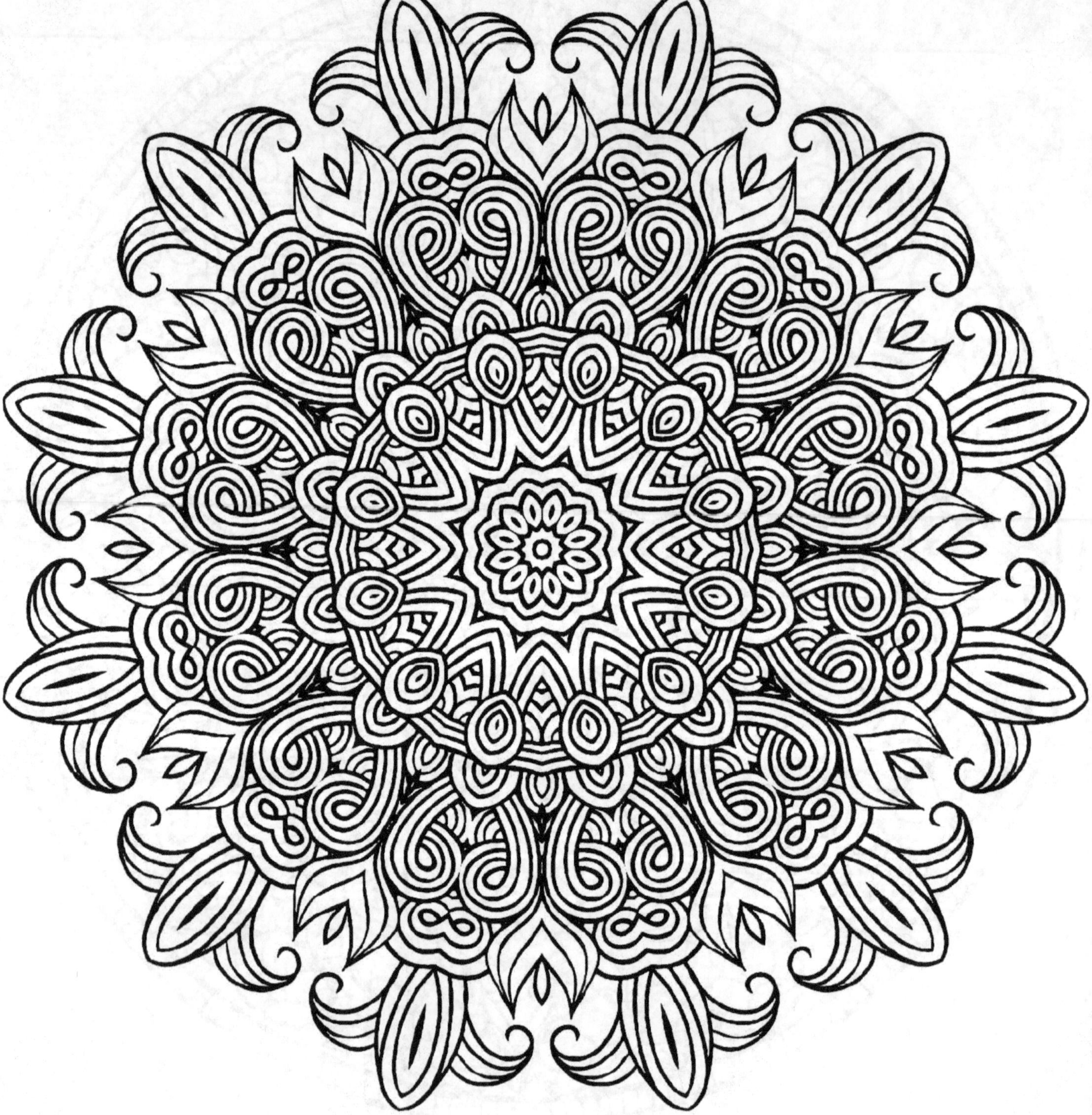

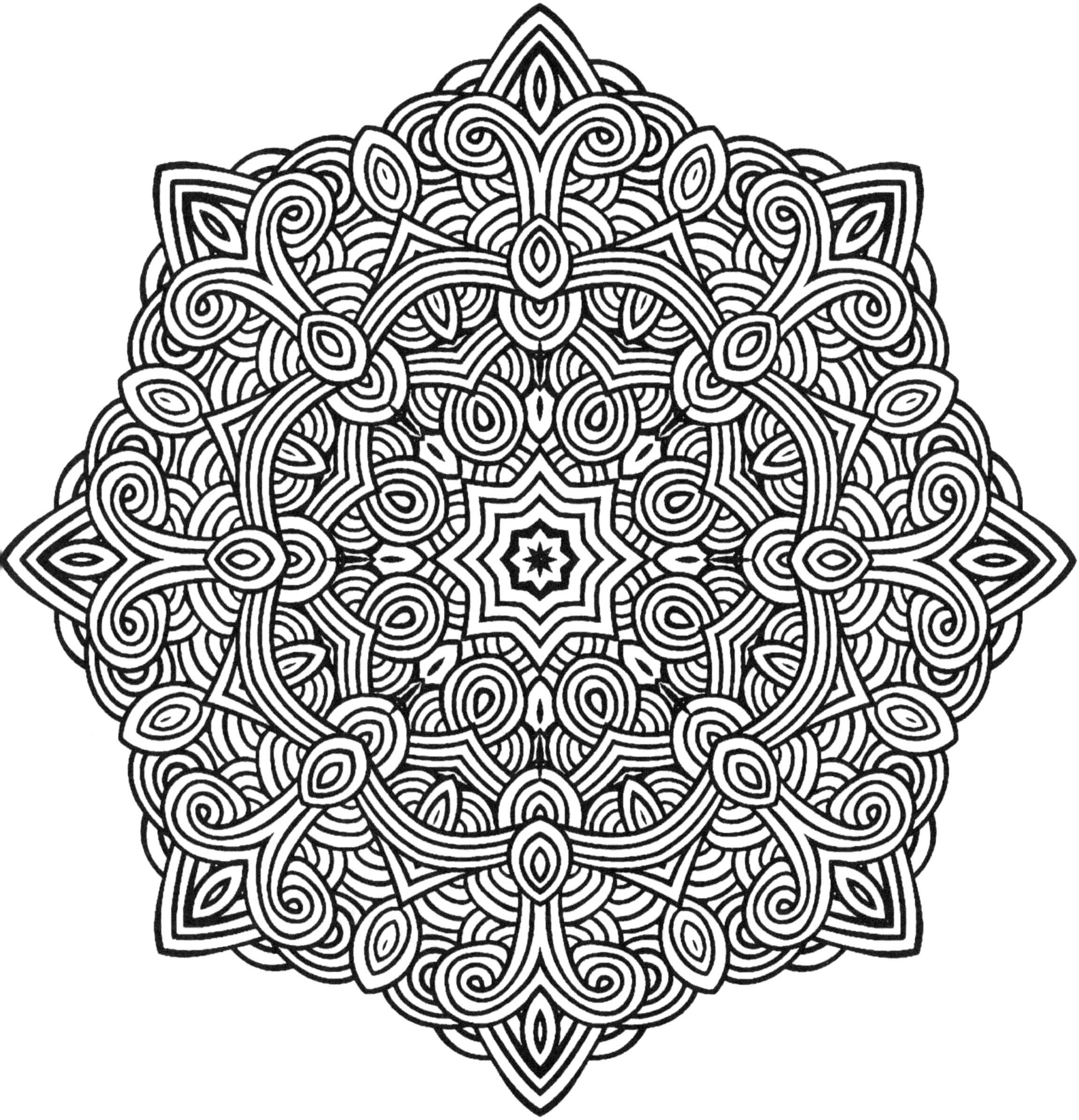

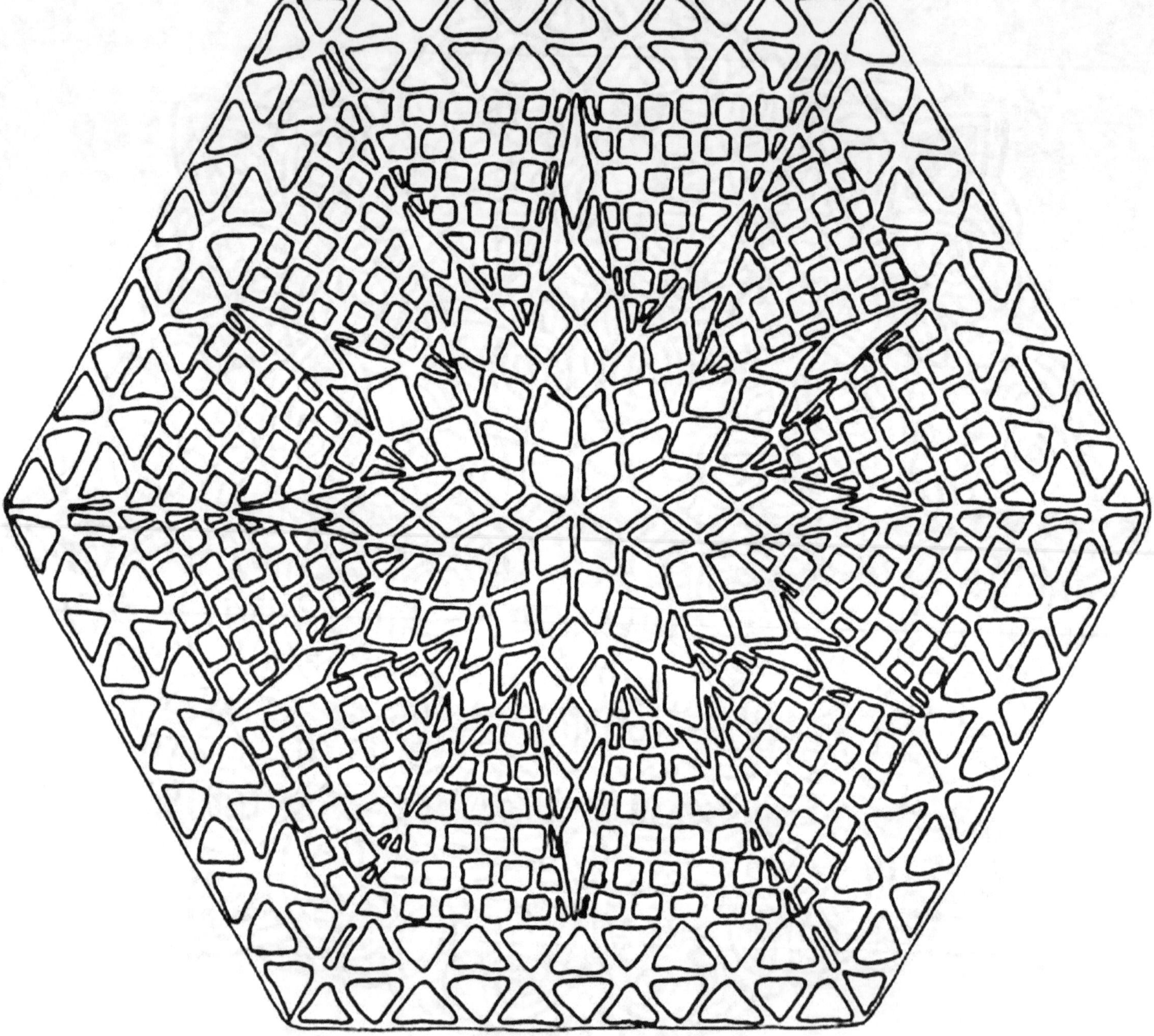

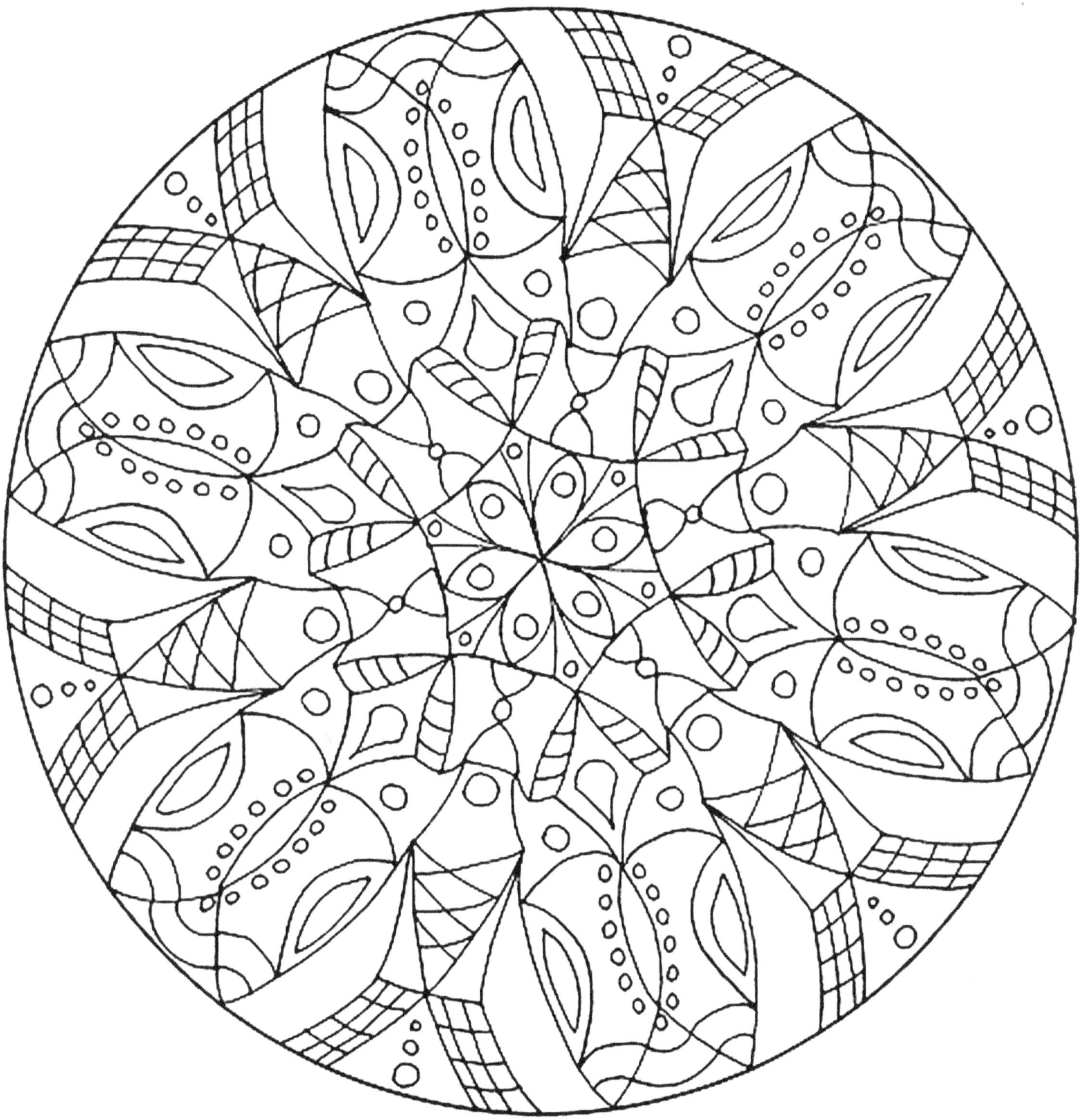

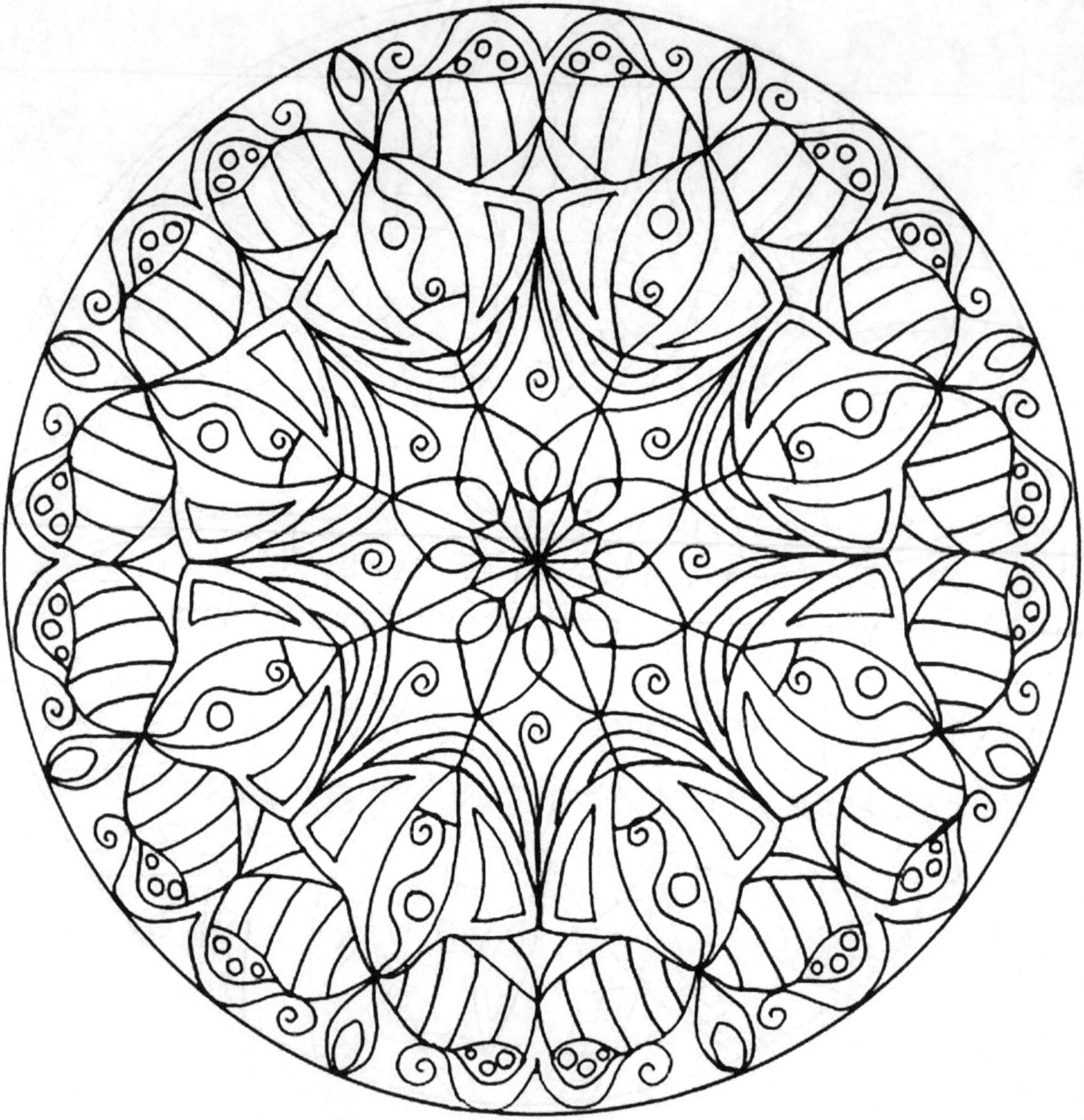

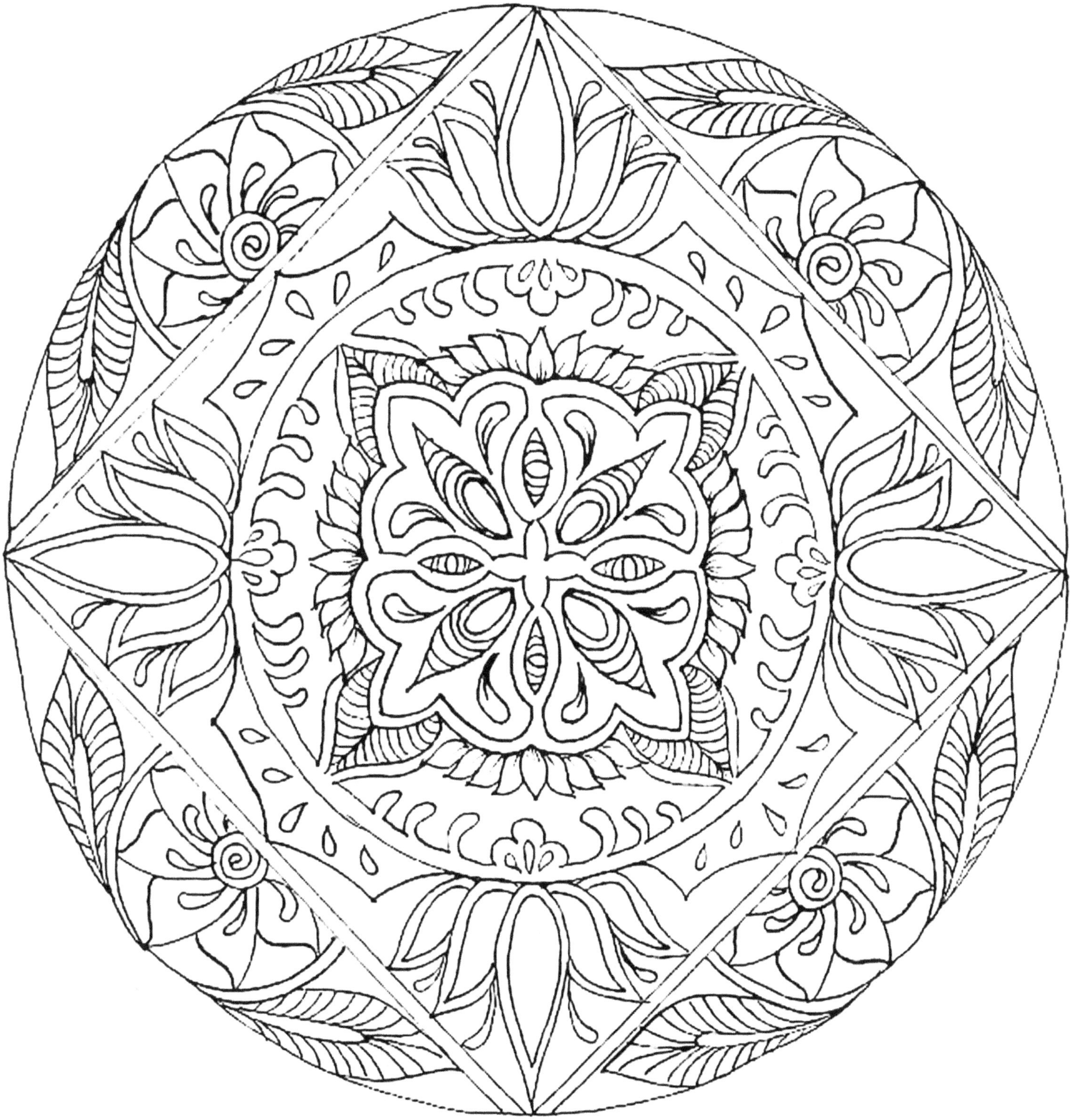

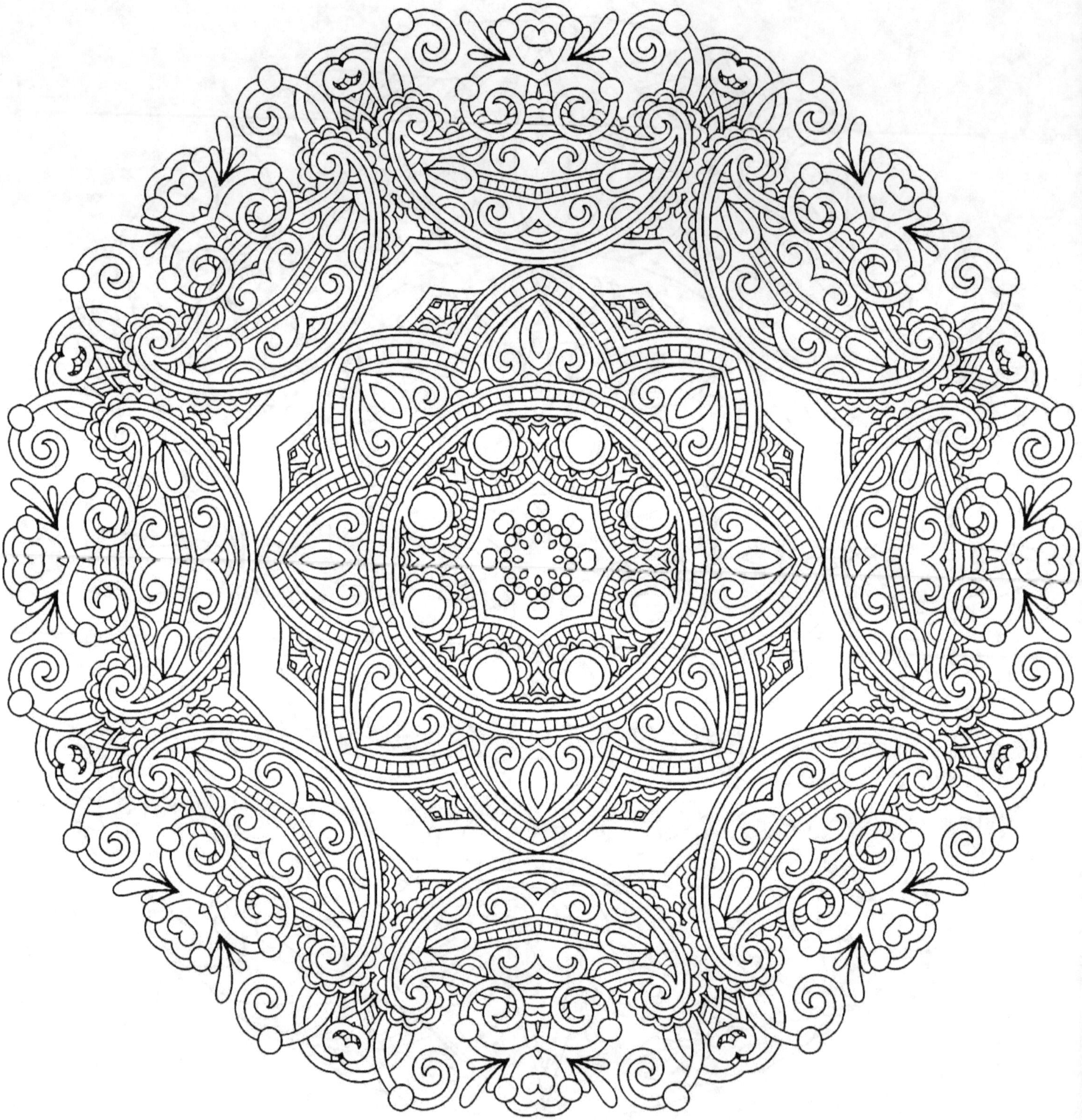

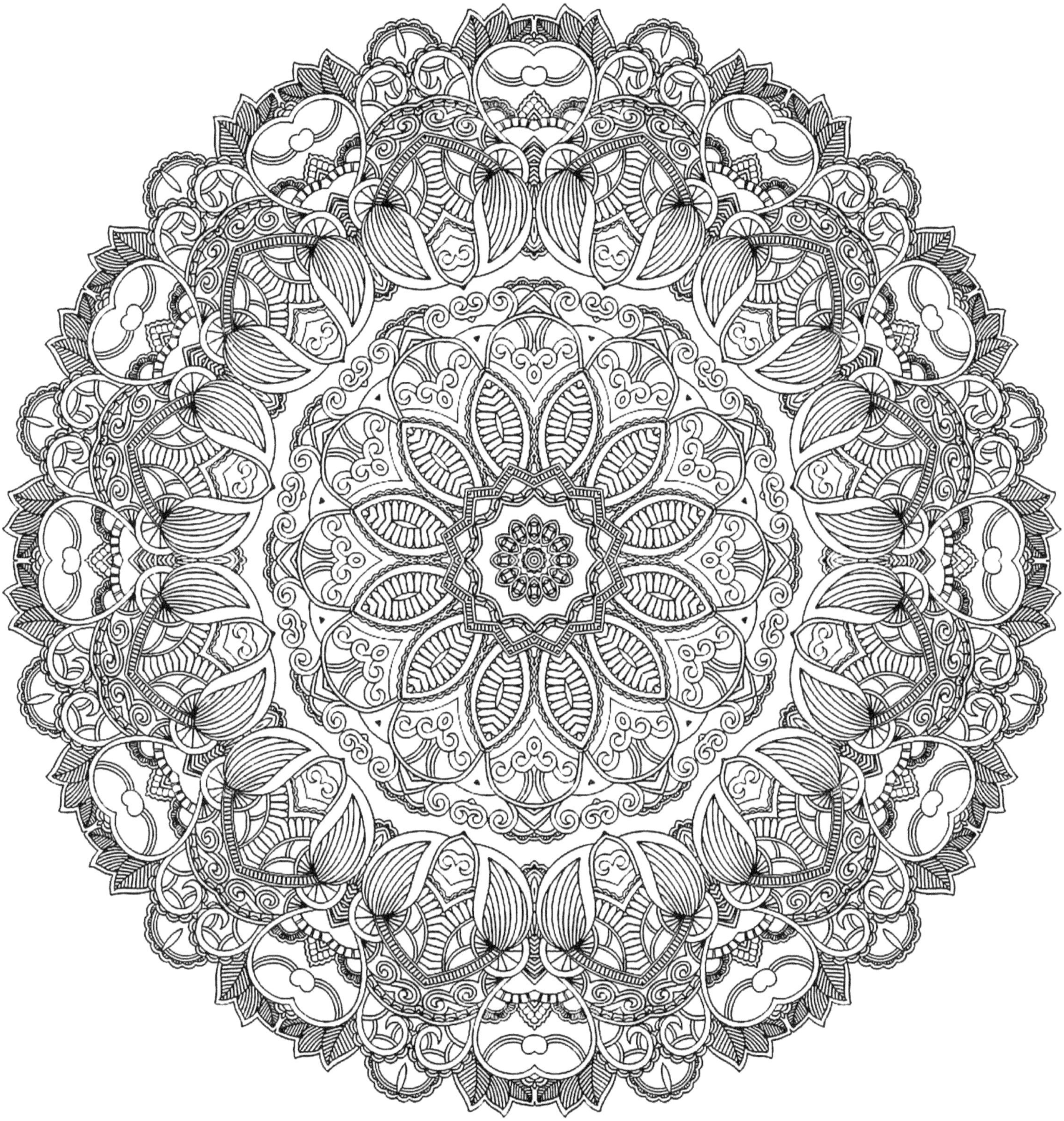

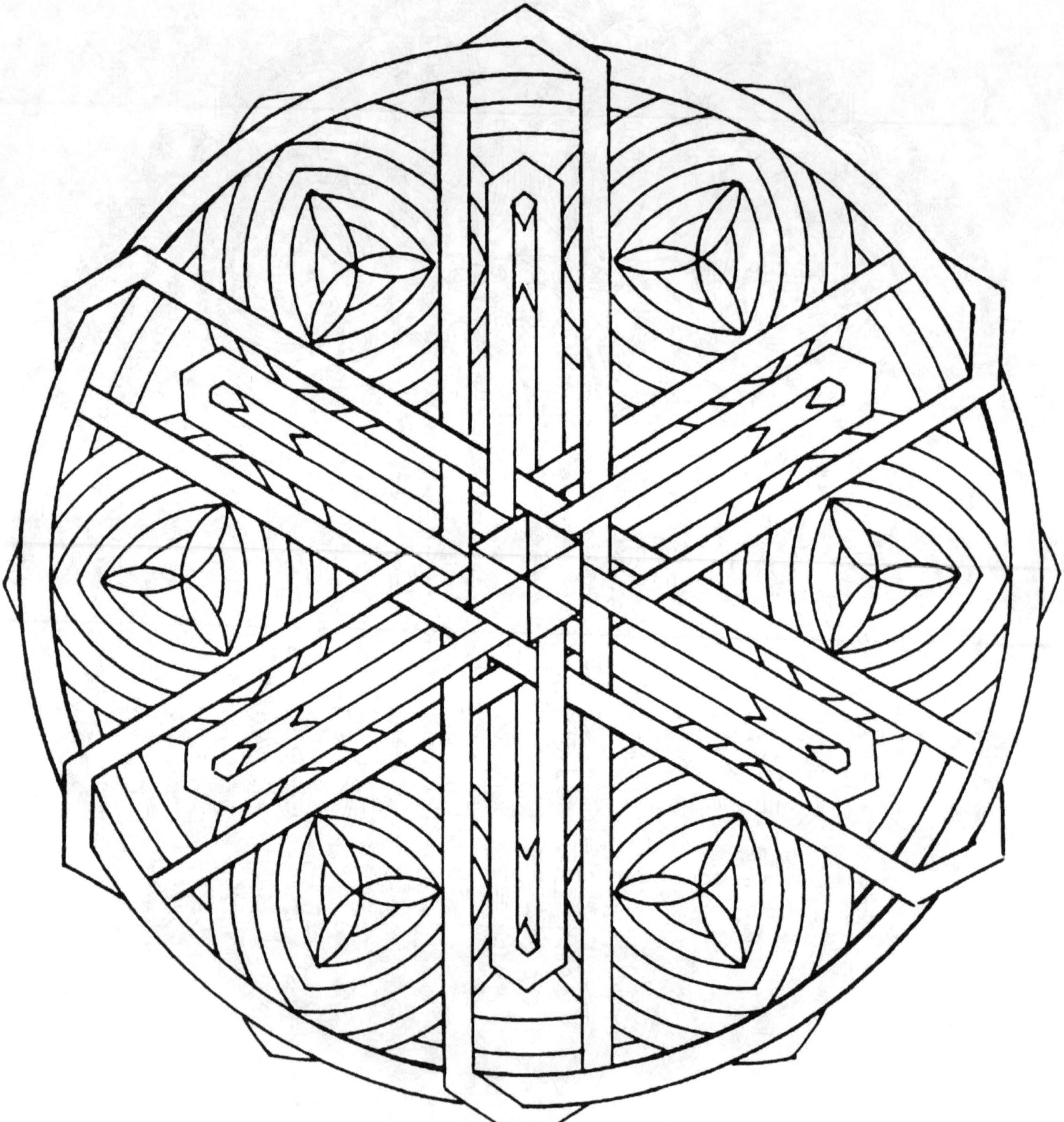

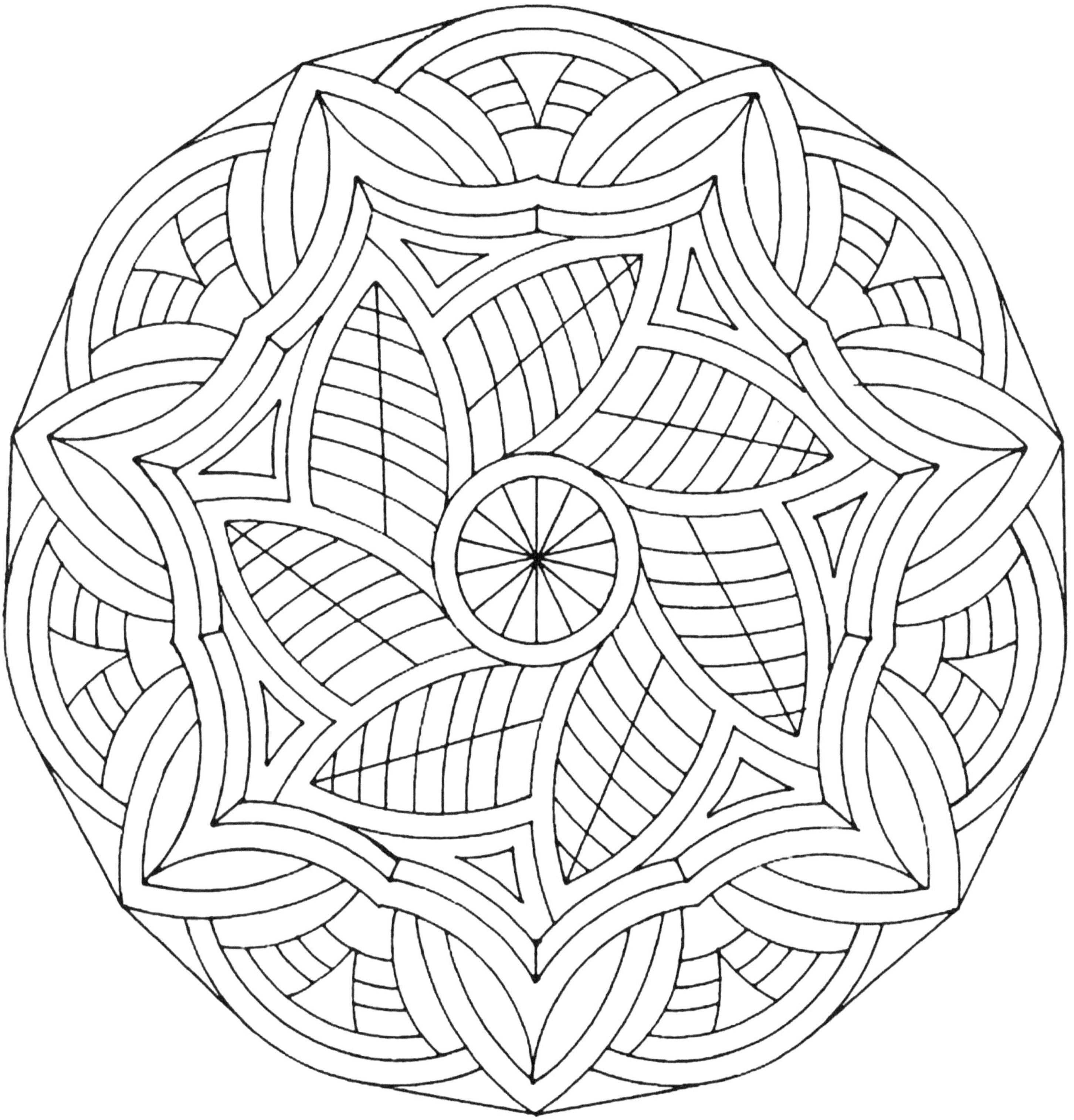

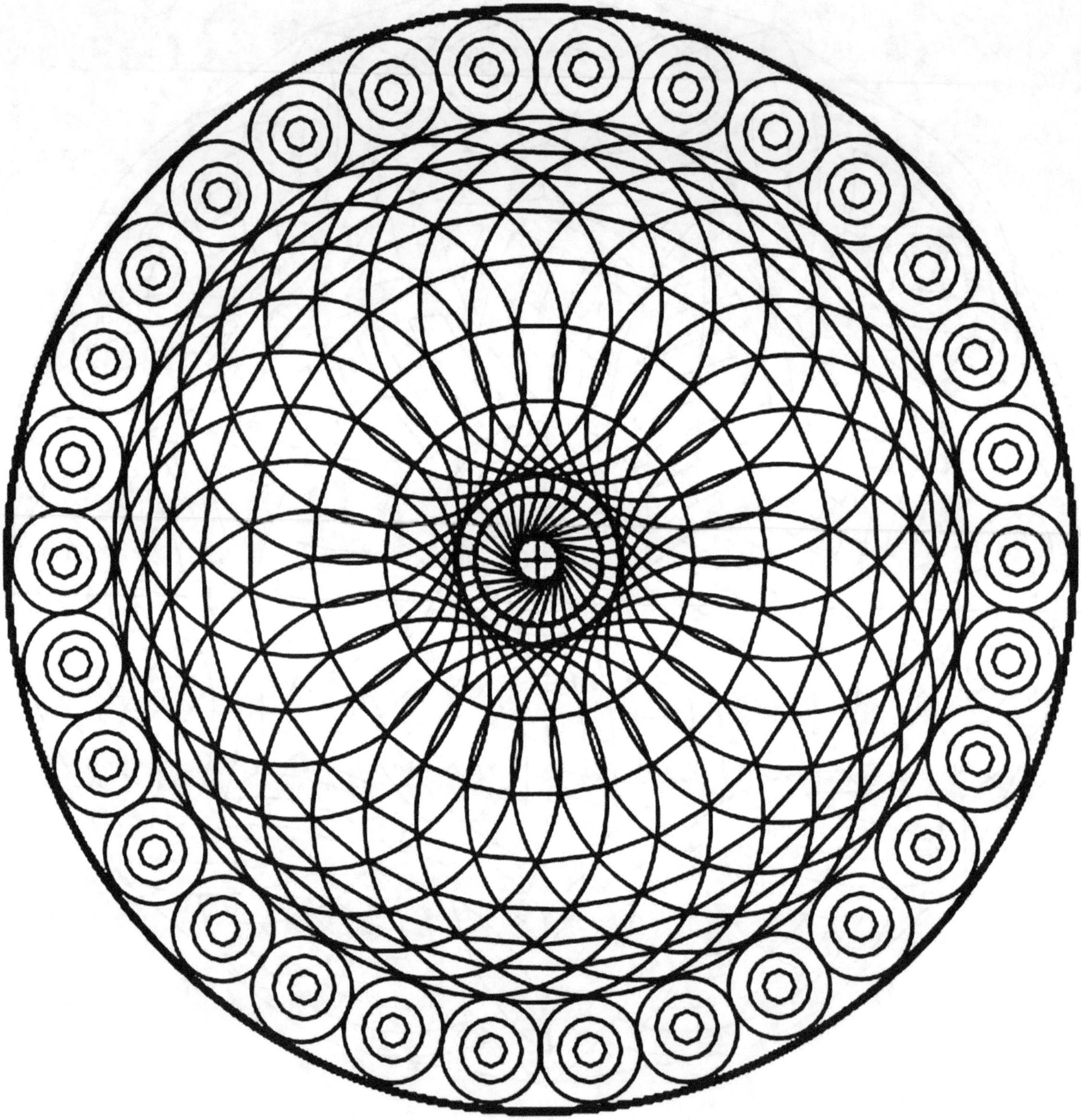

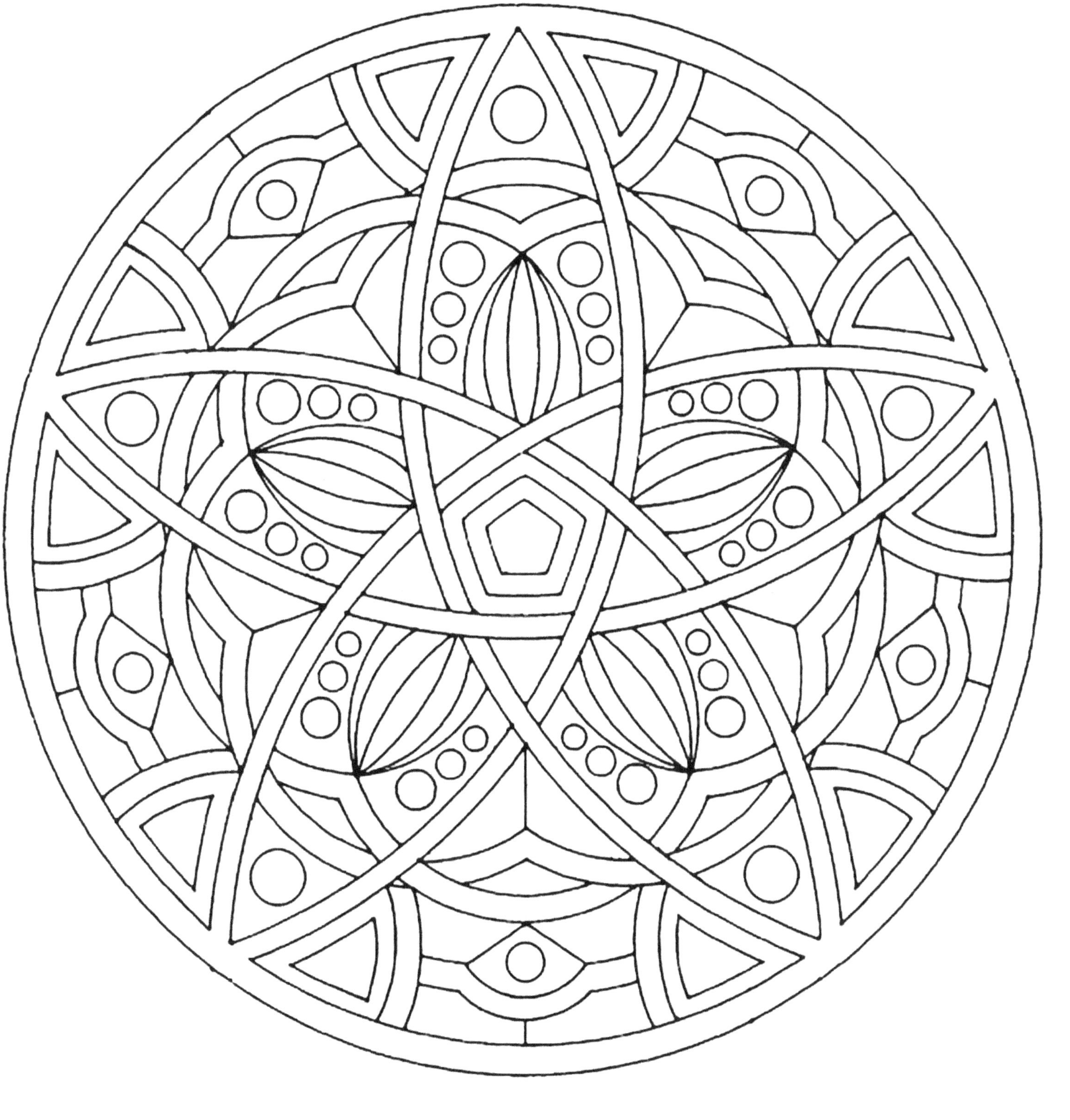

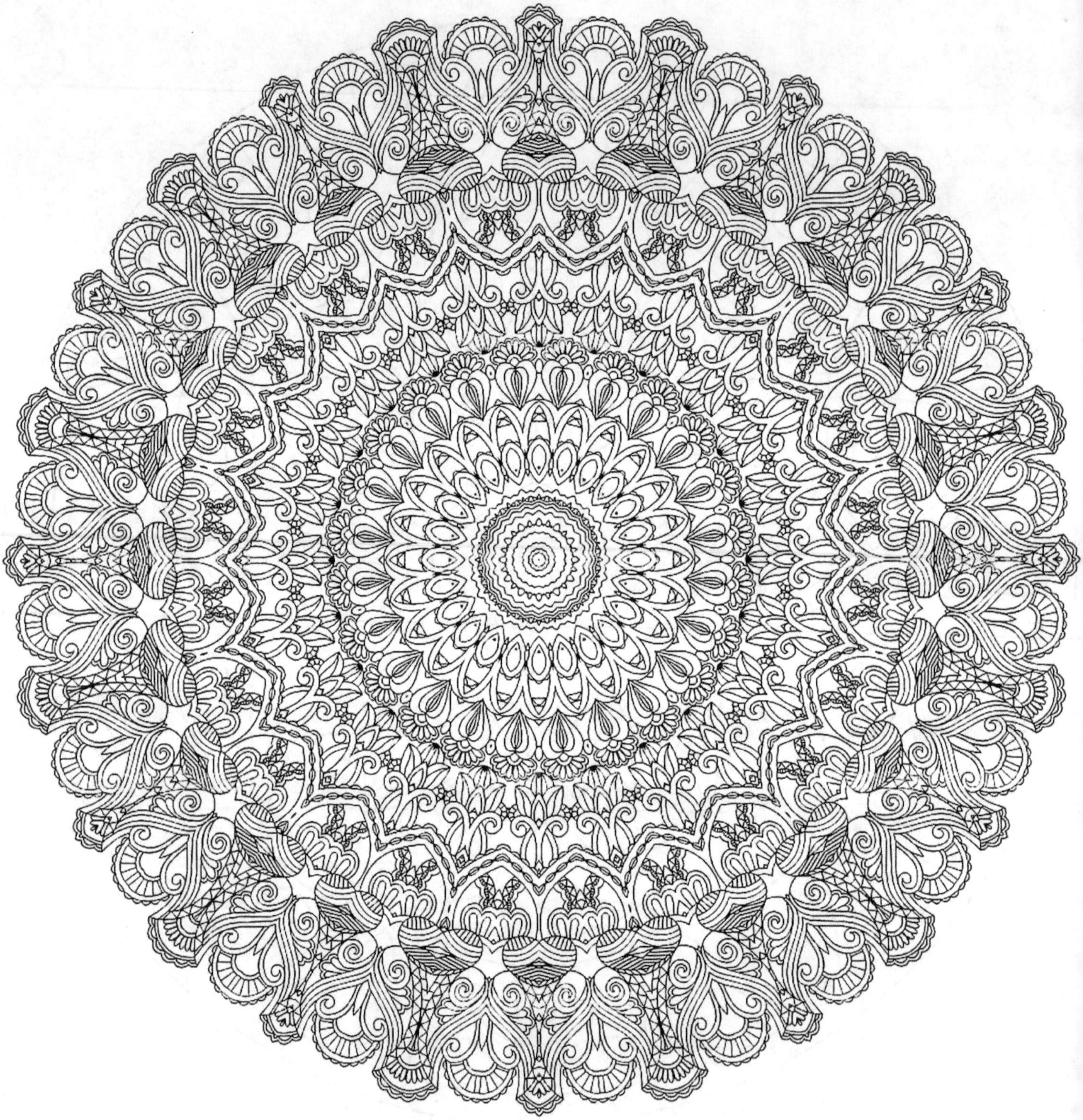

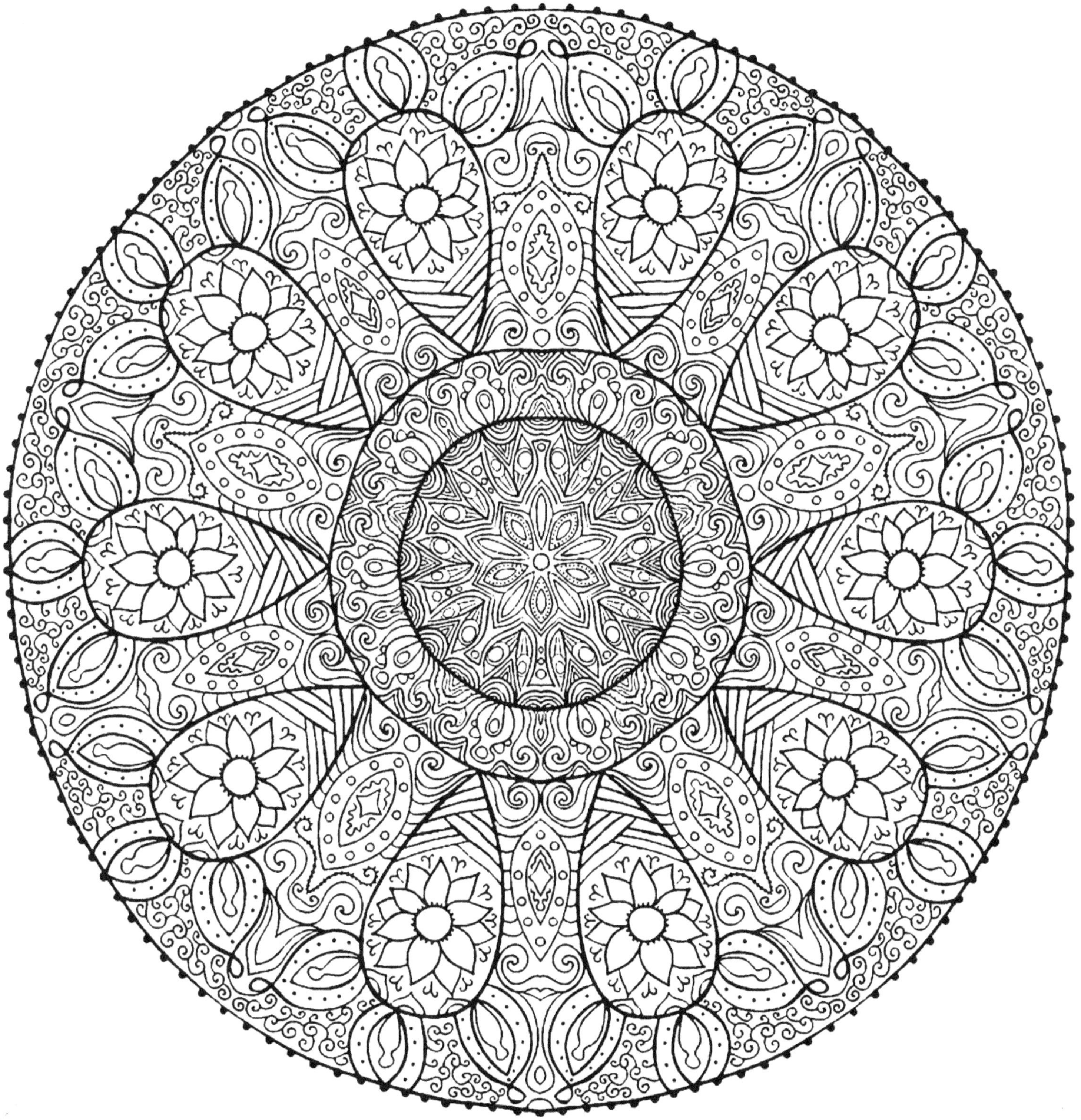

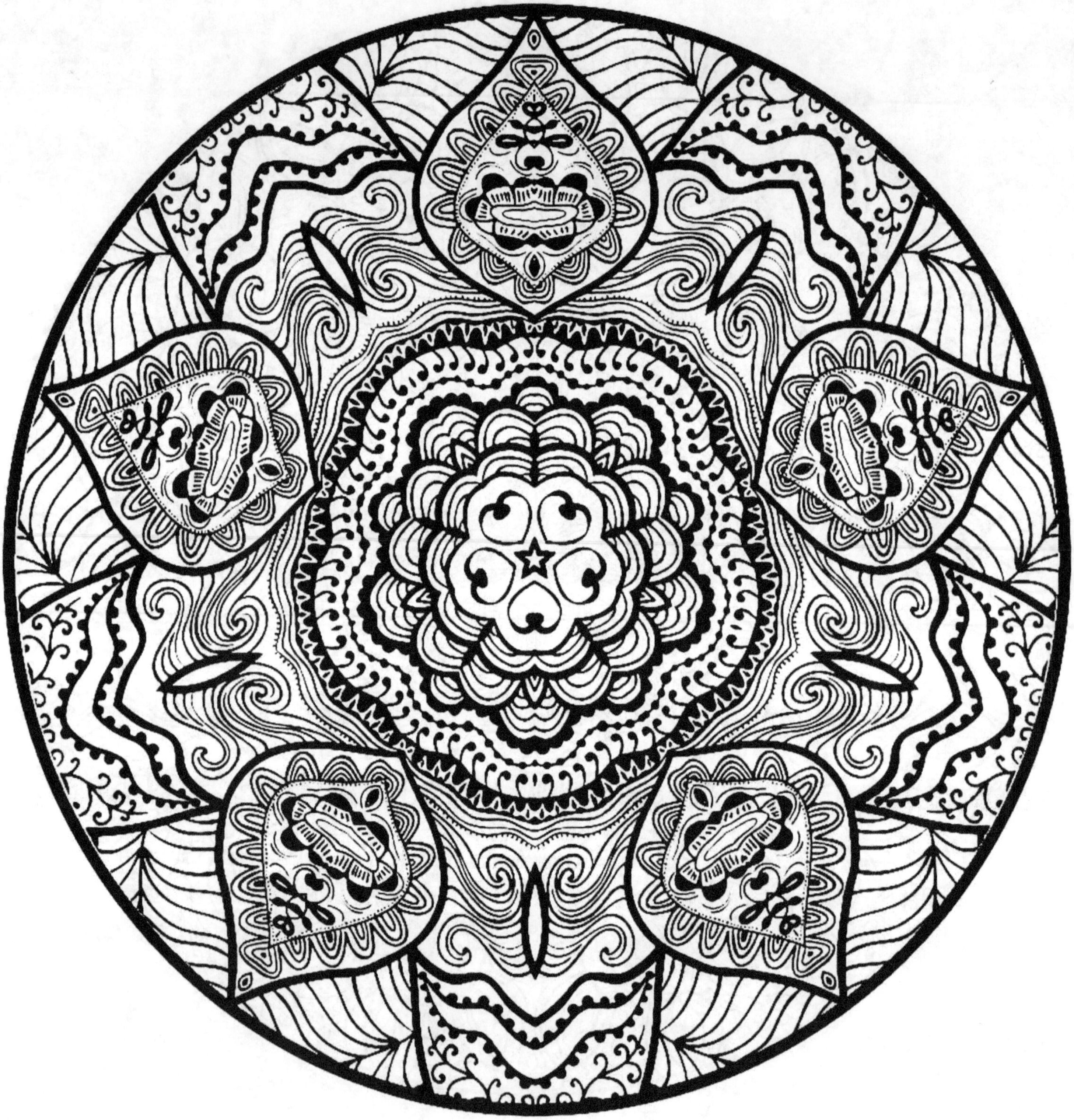

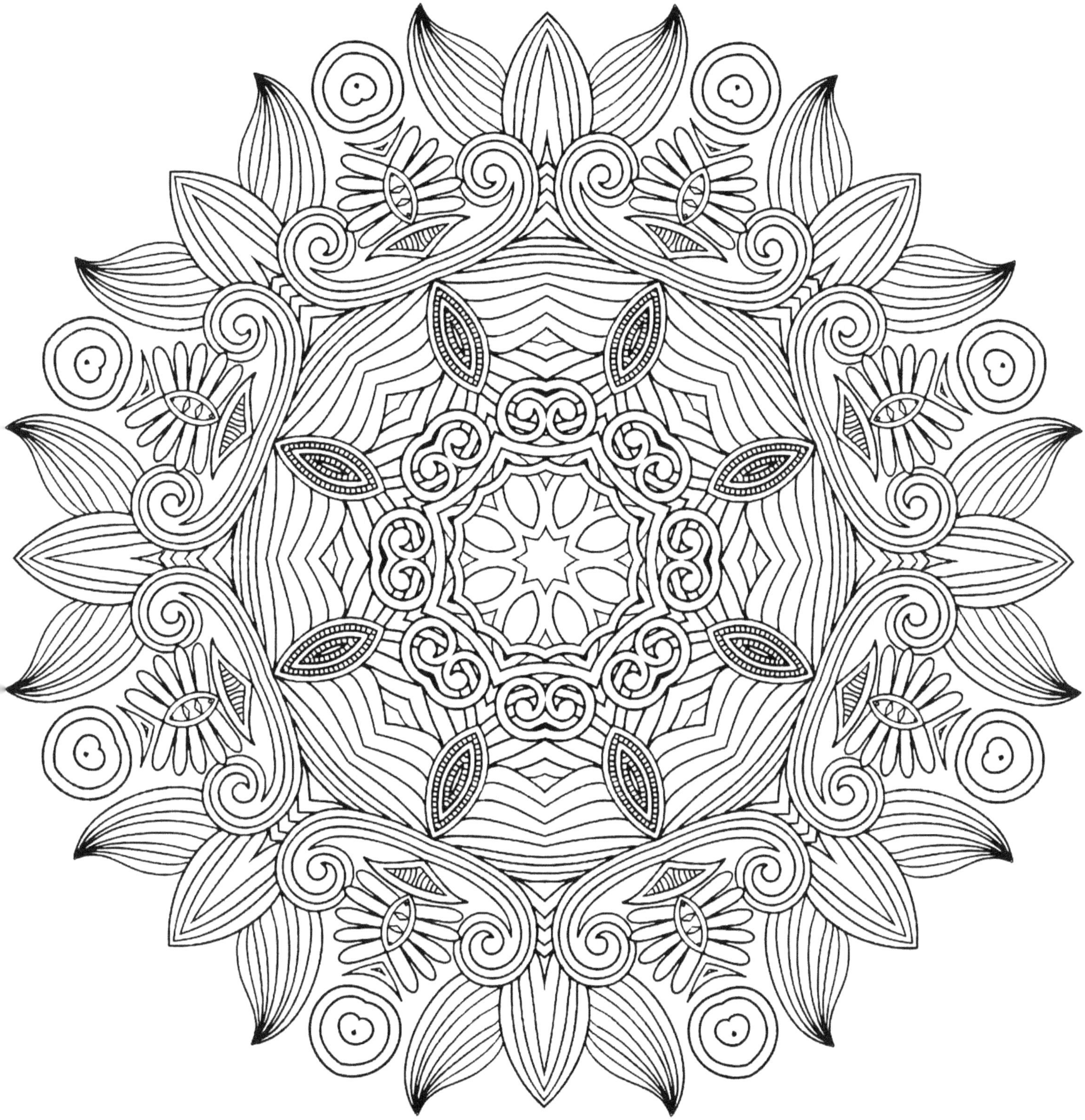

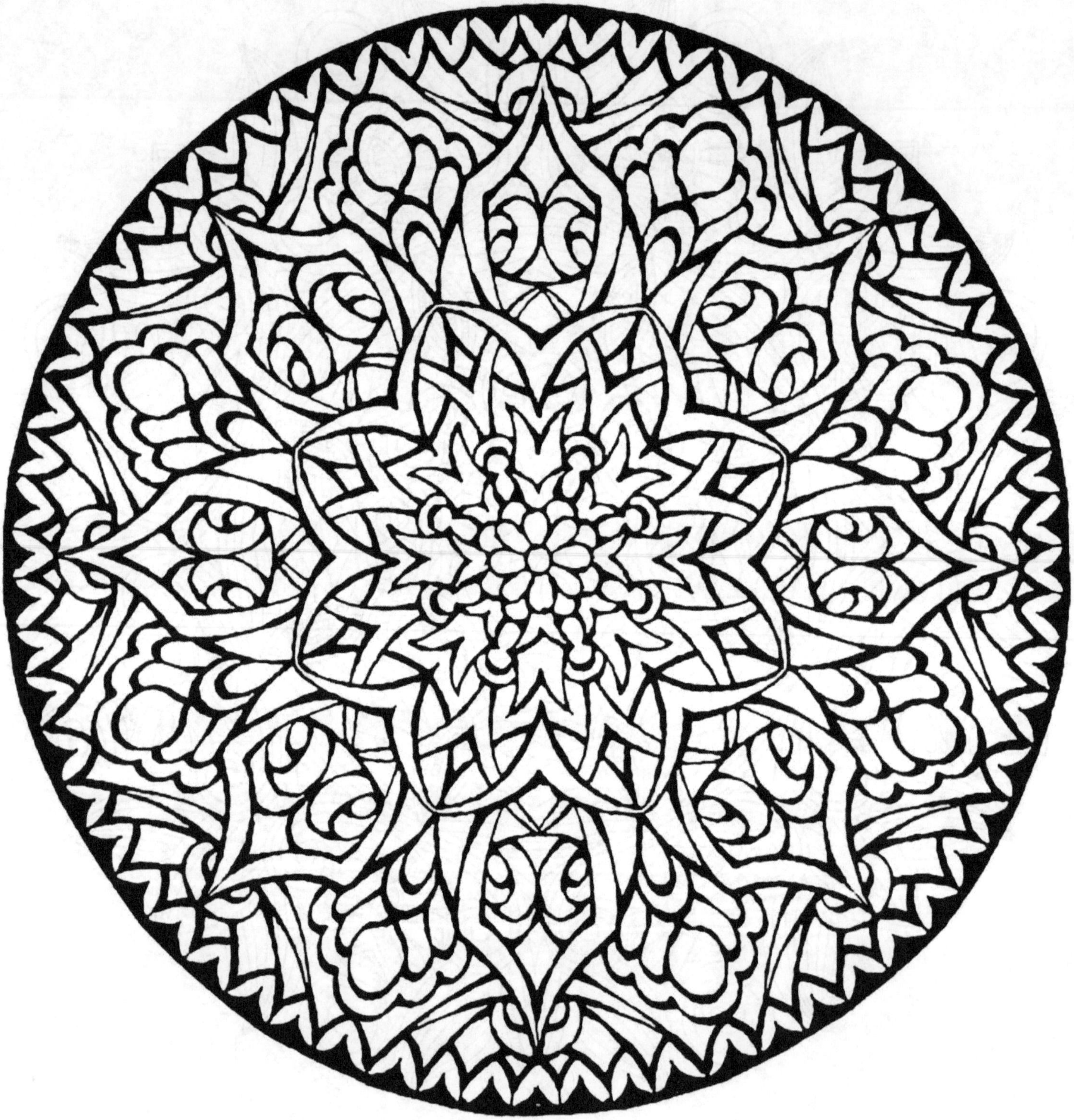

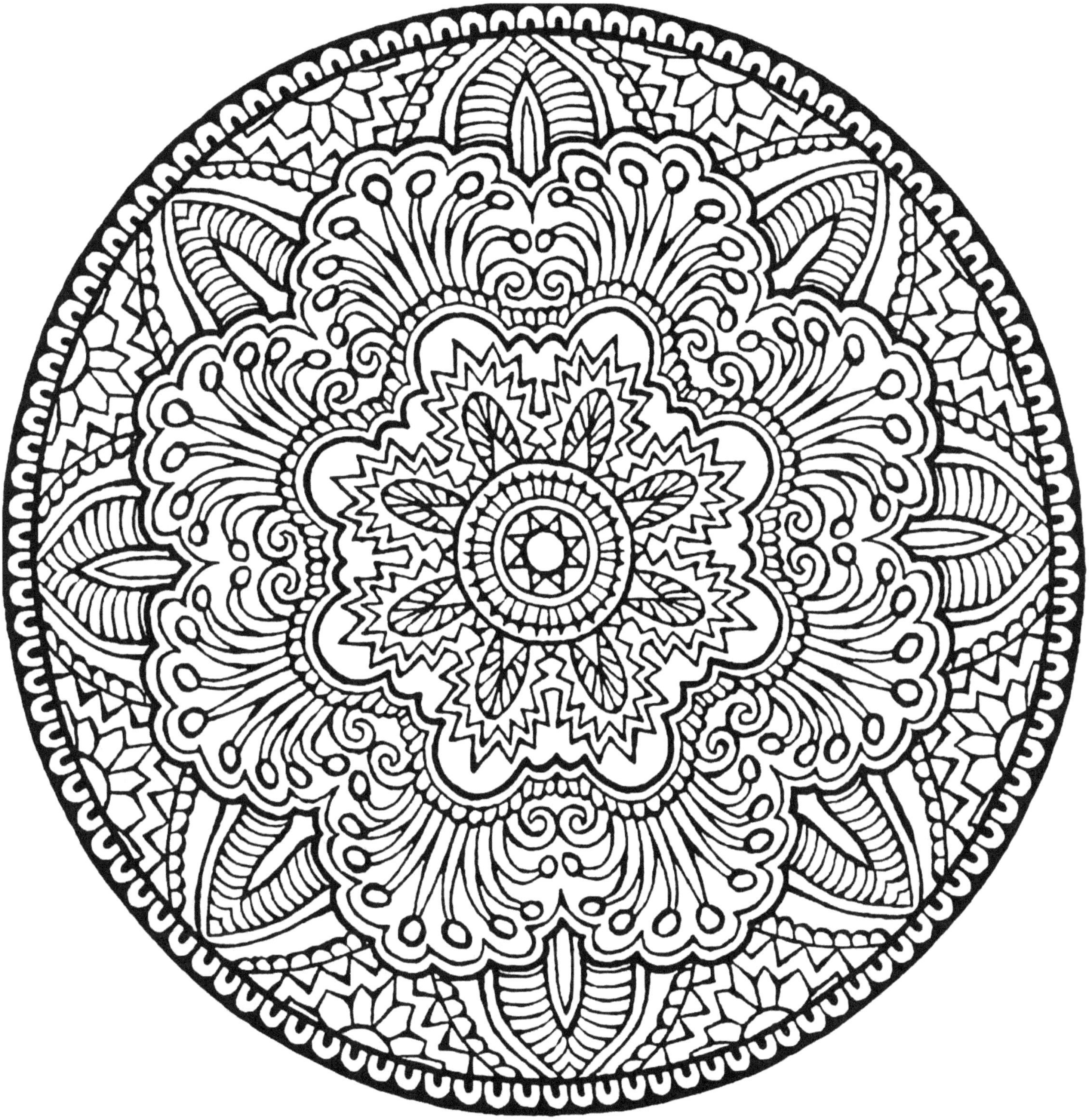

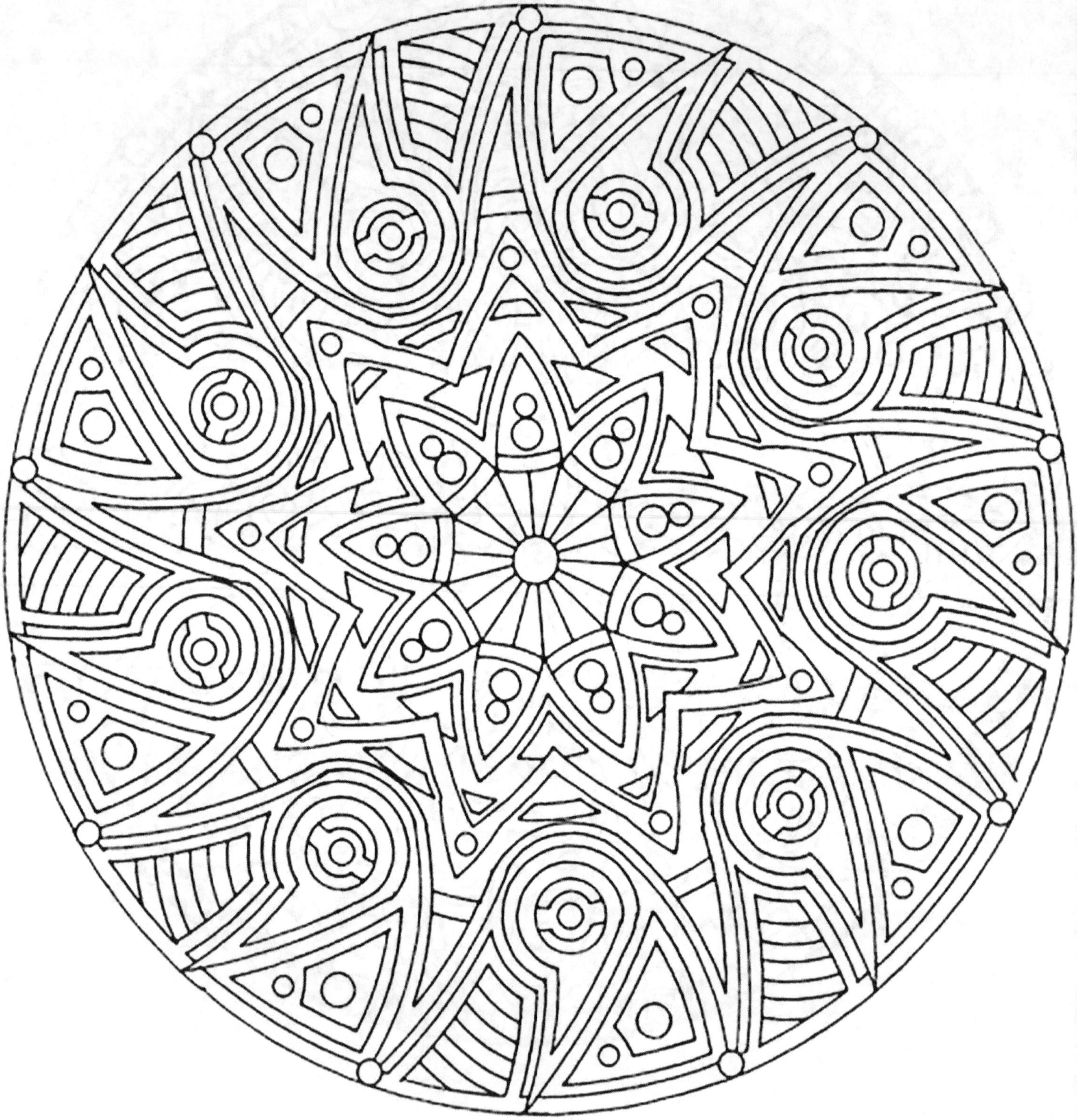

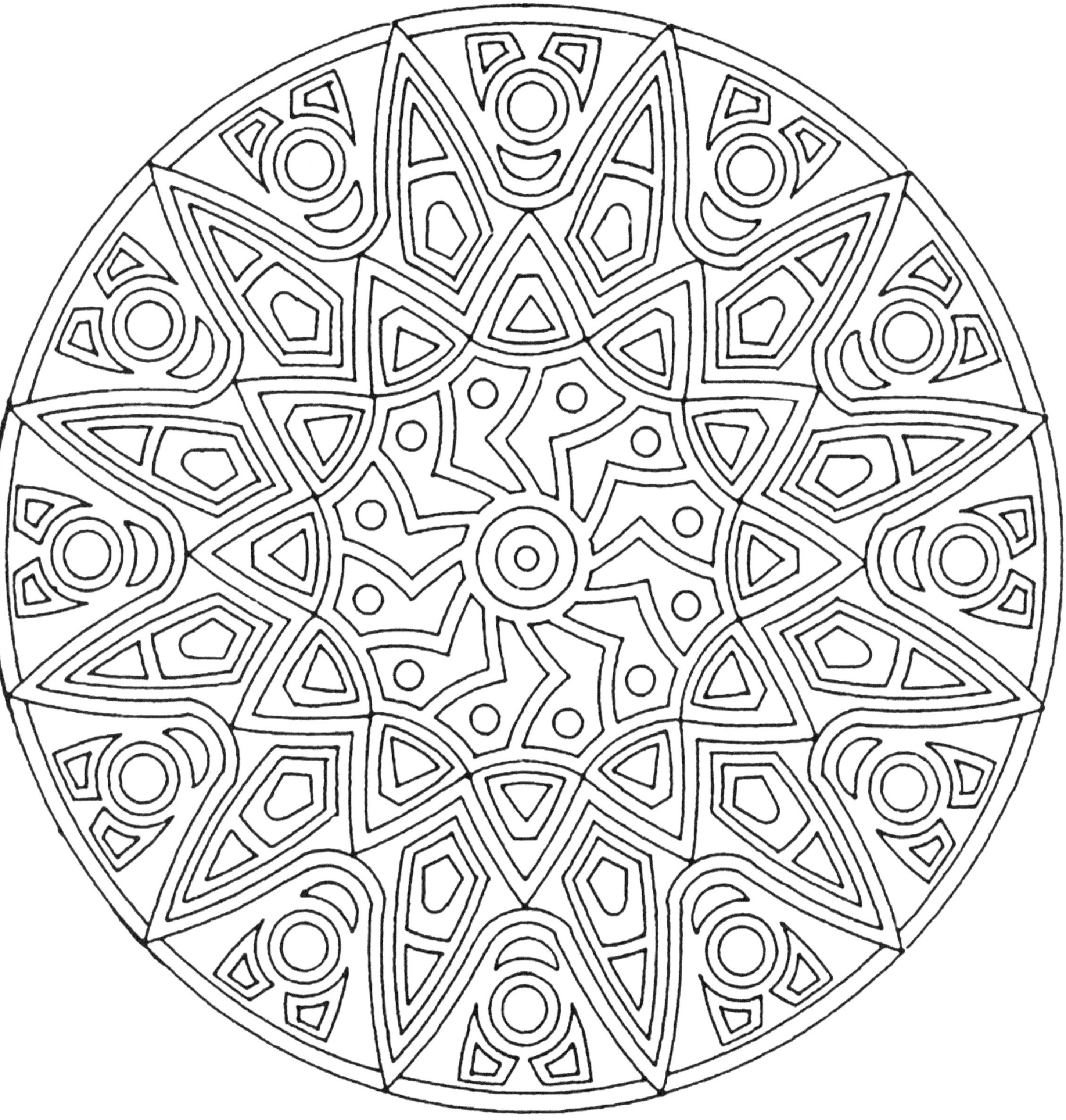

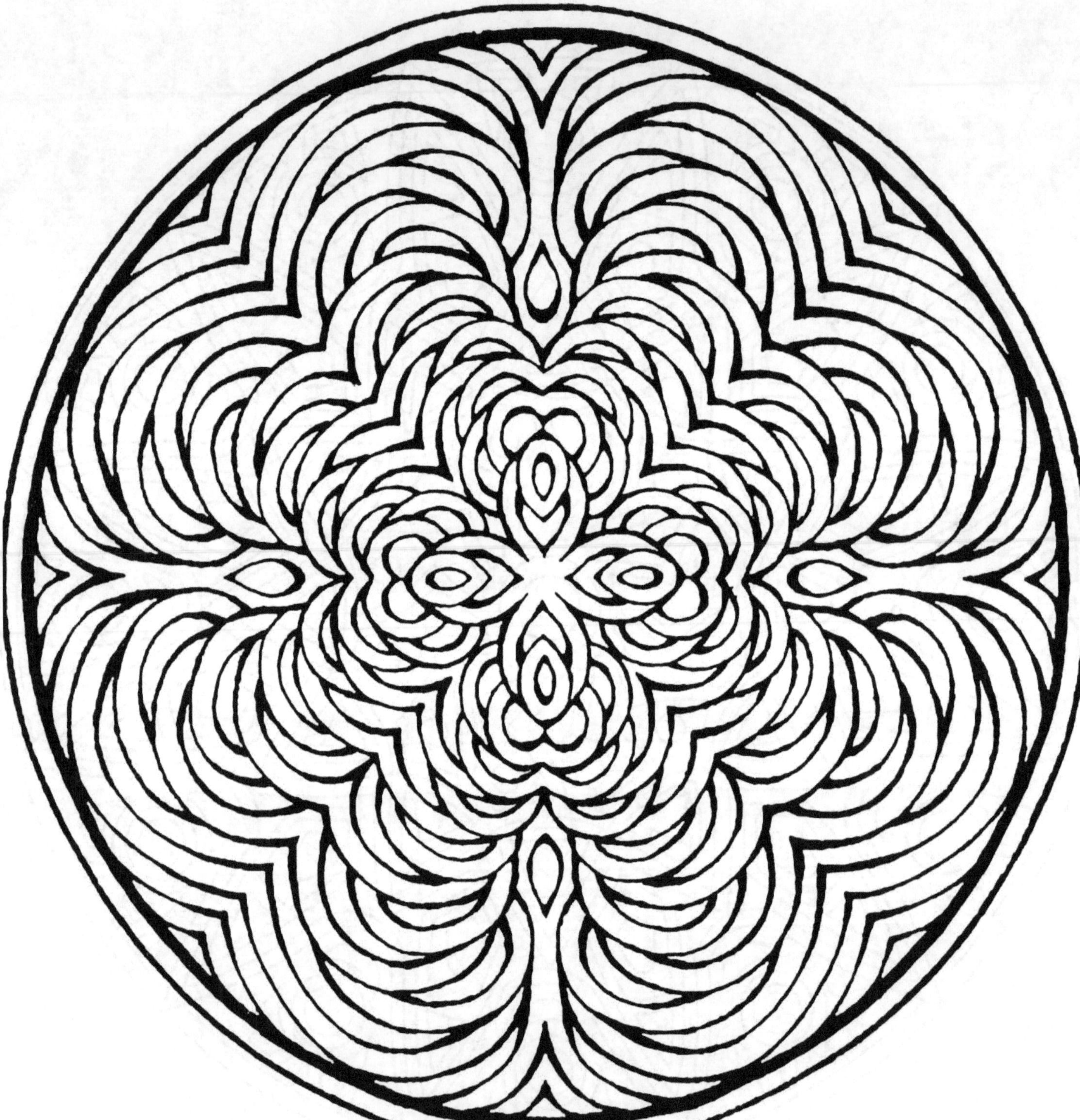

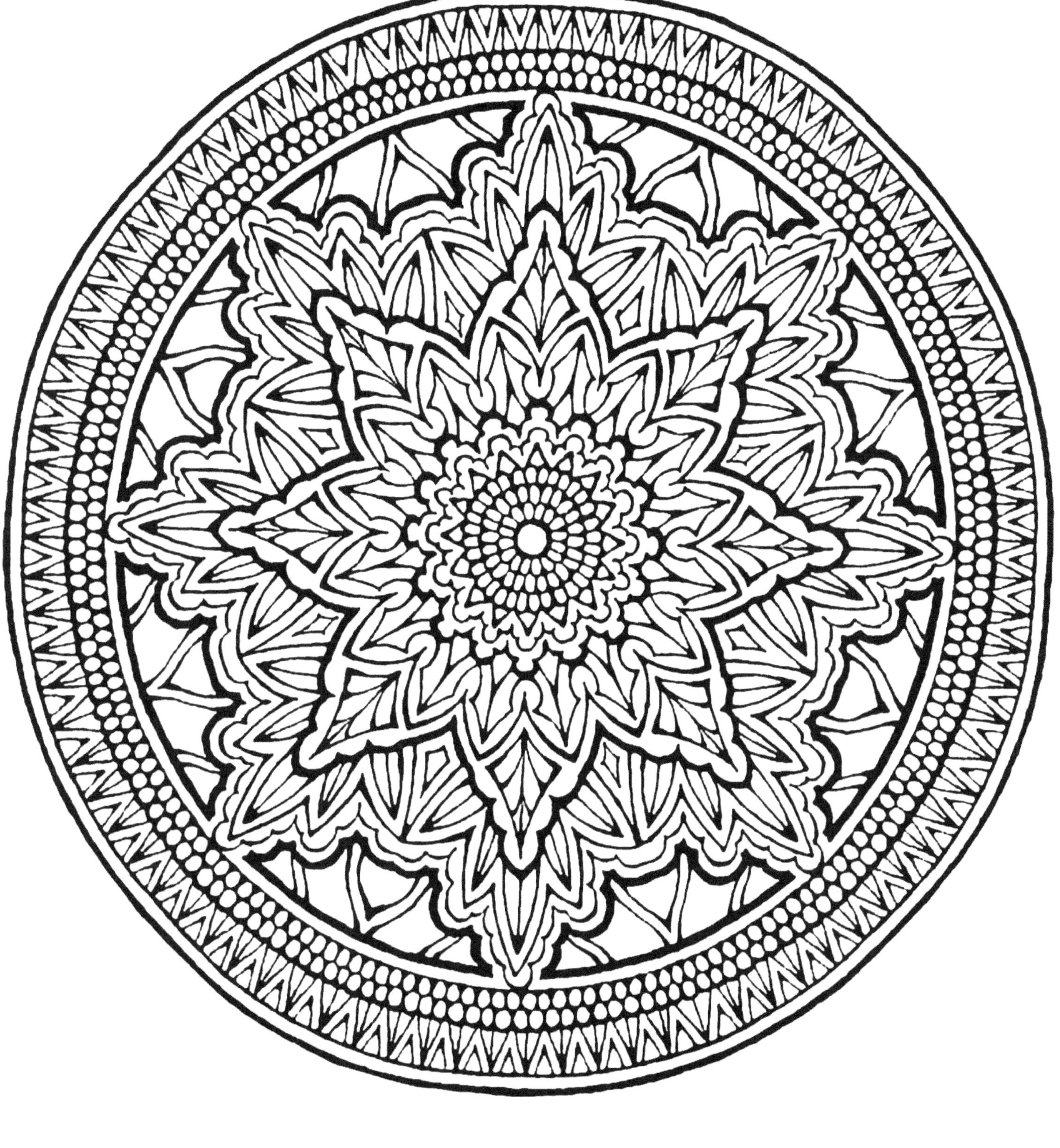

www.ingramcontent.com/pod-product-compliance
Lightning Source LLC
Chambersburg PA
CBHW080555190526
45169CB00007B/2783
* 9 7 8 1 5 2 3 9 9 9 7 8 1 *